LAND ON MY FEET

Rural and Other Encounters
with The Crow

NORMAN MURSELL

Cheshire Country Publishing, Chester

First published in the United Kingdom in 2001
by Cheshire Country Publishing

Copyright © 2001 Cheshire Country Publishing
& Norman Mursell

A catalogue record of this book is
available from the British Library

Land On My Feet

ISBN 0 949001 14 7

INTRODUCTION

IT is twenty years since the publication of Norman Mursell's first book, *Come Dawn, Come Dusk,* in which he captured the very essence of life in the countryside in those halcyon days before the Second World War when, as a young man, he serendipitously moved from the Isle of Wight to commence his entire working life as a game-keeper on the Duke of Westminster's Estate.

Since *Come Dawn, Come Dusk*, Norman has written three other books, all bursting with information, tales, interest and his trademark humour, and all written from the heart, from a countryman who, whether as an author or a raconteur, is so at ease with his subject.

His wisdom and his down-to-earth wit have never been more evident than in *Land On My Feet*.

Here, in his inimitable style and occasionally utilising some of the best stories from his earlier works, he recalls many characters and events, from boyhood adventures fishing the breakwaters of Bembridge Harbour to rural encounters, not only with the future King of England and the great time wartime leader, Winston Churchill, but also with the likes of the parson who had a panache for poaching, the earth-stopper who certainly did not want a medal for his labours, and the General who went fishing with dynamite!

No reader of this fascinating book can fail to be entertained and enlivened by this latest account from the pen of Norman Mursell.

THE AUTHOR
(by Alice Jones)

Quietly he sits and writes
his memories with his pen,
Then takes a rest and lights his pipe,
and blows the smoke, and then.
The smoke twirls round and rises,
Then vanishes in the air,
But all day long the aroma
of tobacco lingers there.
Then from the archives of his mind,
He completes another page,
Full of the wisdom of the years,
From a bygone day and age.
Rarely a day goes by
But he ponders on the past,
And sees how in those years ago
his destiny was cast.
He cannot turn back to alter,
Or remove one iota from its place.
What he has done is done,
No more good can he add, nor evil erase.
He is a humble, kindly man
Who helps all who come his way,
And I wish him health and peace of mind,
Until his dying day.

Youthful Recollections

As a lad, I spent my school years by the seaside, where I was born and coming from a seafaring family, I was quite familiar with the sea in all its moods. The summer was always the best time for us children, practically all the daylight hours being spent on the beach during the school holidays, weather permitting. At other times we were always "down on the shore" for in those days of the 1920s there was much flotsam and jetsam washed up, particularly on an easterly wind which brought all sorts down the English Channel.

Once, when walking along the beach with the tide almost at the high, my friend and I came across numerous small round tins, with their seals unbroken and, curiosity overcoming us, we broke one open to discover that it held cigarettes. There were no labels on the tins and clearly they had been in the water for some considerable time, but the tobacco was completely dry and undamaged. Fifty cigarettes in each tin there were and we finished up with almost a sackful, the sack having been "borrowed" out of a small fishing boat hauled up on the beach. We were fine and excited but we had no idea what to do with our "treasure". There was not a soul to be seen, a rather unusual state of affairs, for the older retired fishermen were seldom off the beach. There was only one thing to do; take them home.

At this particular time, my father was at sea, on a yacht sailing around the Italian coast, and all my mother wanted was for us to "bury them". "No fear," my friend, a certain Jack Mursell (no relation) said. "We'll leave them in your shed. If I take them to our house the old chap will collar them and smoke the lot. I reckon we can get a bit of pocket money out of our find."

A day or two passed and then whilst we were talking to some older boys, someone said: "There's been a few fags washed up," whereupon Jack replied: "We've got hundreds," which we had. "Give us some," said one of teenagers. "Not likely," was our reply. "We'll sell you some!".

A bargain was struck. "Threepence a tin!" There was some argument over this, of course, but fifty for three-pence had to be a bargain. As the days passed, our supply of fags got less and less and the money in our pockets more and more, even men were coming for a tin, for word had got round. We had almost disposed of all the tins when the village policeman called. He had heard that we were selling cheap cigarettes and asked us where we had got them from. We explained what had happened and all about our find on the tide line, which he expected, but then told us that we should have reported our find to the Coastguard who would have then contacted the Customs officer for the district. Jack said: "What would have happened then?". "Oh all the tins would have been confiscated," said the bobby. "Then we would have got nothing," said Jack. "Quite correct. How many have you got left?" the policeman queried. "Only three," we told him.

"Well I'll have a couple," came the reply, "but don't for-get, if you find any more it must be reported and be good lads and let me know before you tell the Coastguard." With that away he went. Jack wasn't too impressed:

"Well blow me, he didn't pay, he owes us a tanner!".

Needless to say, we never did find any more tins of cigarettes on the shore when we were beachcombing, but that was certainly a most profitable encounter.

In those far off days, lads always found something to occupy their out-of-school hours and the pastimes were varied. In the spring of the year, birds' nesting was a favourite hobby, for it was not breaking the law to take eggs in those days and many a lad had quite a large collection. During my youth, which perhaps I should say was spent on the Isle of Wight at Bembridge, there lived in the village what seemed to us an "old gentleman", one Gerry Goodall, who had spent much of his life in the Argentine having "jumped" ship as a youth. He must have done well for himself for he owned a number of nitrate mines and when he retired he built a large bungalow which he named "The Nest". He spent much of his time fishing and collecting birds' eggs and he had, apparently, brought a large number of eggs home with him from South America. He was always pleased when a village lad called and told him about an unusual nest and there was, of course, always a copper or so for providing the information.

This naturally made for intense activity amongst the village youth when the birds, many of them migratory, startled nesting. One summer's evening a pal and myself were on a nesting expedition, in fact looking for a Lesser Whitethroat's nest. The common "Peggy" Whitethroat was plentiful, but its cousin the "Lesser" was quite rare. We had seen the cock Lesser Whitethroat busy feeding amongst the shrubs in the grounds of a large private residence and, with what we thought was youthful cunning, decided to try to find the nest whilst the occupier of the house was having an evening meal. In we crept through a gap in the hedge and, with some trepidation, started to search for the small well-built nest that we were certain was present in the herbage. After only about five minutes, we were peering in a rather dense patch when a voice right behind us said:

7

"What do you think you two lads are doing?".

We were startled but didn't run away. In fact, the gentleman was in such a position that it was impossible for us to do so. It was obvious that we were searching for nests and so we confessed all to the gentleman with a ruddy face and white hair.

Fortunately he was not at all irate and when we told him our names, he said: "Oh your family is well known in this community. I see no reason why you shouldn't look for nests in my garden." He then proceeded to help us search the shrubbery until we found the elusive nest. We then told him we would like Mr Gerry Goodall to know about it and he was delighted. "Go and tell him, he's a great friend of mine," he said. "You may come into my garden (it was about an acre!) anytime you like, but always knock on the door first."

Off we went to "The Nest" to find Mr Goodall who was pottering in the garden and, no doubt, guessed the purpose of our visit.

"What is your spectacular achievement now lads?" he greeted us with. We thereupon told him about the Lesser Whitethroat's nest, the large house on the outskirts of the village and the kindly gentleman who had given us permission to go nesting in his garden.

Mr Goodall seemed to consider this situation for a while and then said, "Well you must learn a lesson from this, for a good name is worth gold, yea, more than much gold. If you always remember this it will stand you in good stead as you go through life."

These were wise words from a wise man over sixty years ago and I have always remembered them.

Talking of birds' nesting there was, in the vicinity of the village, a vast tract of marshy ground, two thousand acres or more. It had been reclaimed from the sea fifty or so years earlier and contained "dry" land, where cattle were normally grazed, and also lagoons, nearly all of which were fringed by tall rushes. The whole area was ideal for wildlife and the drier areas, although these were quite boggy in places, became the breeding ground of the lapwing, many hundreds of pairs nesting there at one time. The lagoons were favoured by coot, moorhen, mallard and smaller birds, mostly migratory, that came to breed in the spring. In the winter, of course, there were larger areas of water and many wildfowl used the area as a "staging" post. There was also also an amazing diversity of flora, ranging from several types of orchids to numerous types of rushes, and it was altogether an area of great interest to naturalists.

Rivalry amongst the birds nesting lads of the village was often quite intense over who had the best egg collection, i.e. who had the most eggs or who had eggs from the most species. There were also some lads who were aloof from such rivalry, preferring instead to concentrate on the different colouration of eggs from just one or two species, for instance blackbird, mistle thrush or reed warbler.

We decided to look for nests on the marshy ground, my pal being keen to build up his collection of reed warblers' eggs for although one hen bird's egg is rarely identical to another, at least when the eggs are mottled, or marked, in a scrawly fashion, it was difficult to find any quantity that showed great variation. He would take the entire clutch of eggs, and had eight or nine clutches in his collection, as often there would only be one egg different from the others.

It was not difficult to locate the area where the warblers were nesting for the "sweet and harsh" notes of the cock bird could be heard from some distance and now and again a bird would hover above the reeds. The water in most of the lagoons was quite shallow, hardly knee-deep, so it was possible to get to many of the nests providing you were wearing rubber boots and, anyway, we were quite prepared to remove our footwear if necessary.

The nests themselves were not always easy to distinguish, normally suspended two to three feet above the water and built around three or more tall rushes. The nests, made from the feathery remains of the previous year's rush seedheads, were not very substantial and it was possible to see daylight through them.

Soon we found a couple of clutches of warblers' eggs that appeared to be different and also one nest with what we were sure was a cuckoo's egg within the clutch. At the same time we gathered coots' and moorhens' eggs, as they were good for eating, either boiled or in a cake.

On the way home, the coots' and moorhens' eggs carried in the peaks or our caps, a detour had to be made to walk along some higher dry ground and we were chatting happily, until we passed a small clump of gorse which proved to be the hiding place of the gamekeeper.

"What have you two been up to?" he asked.

"Only taking a walk," was the reply.

"More than that I think," said the keeper who had clearly been watching us for some time.

"How many birds' nests have you robbed?"

"We've only looked at one or two," said my pal.

"Come on hand them over," said the keeper.

"We haven't got any," I replied.

"Ah well we had better find out," said Old Velveteens as he stepped forward, slapped our pockets and tapped us on the front of the head. The eggs were smashed and, much to our dismay, the contents started to trickle down our faces. "Funny that, considering you said you hadn't touched any eggs," he said. "Now get off with you and don't come down on this land again."

We departed rapidly with those words ringing in our ears, but of course after a few days the attraction of birds nesting became too great and the marshes had to be re-visited, but in future we were always on the look-out for that keeper. We knew full well that another such encounter would have more dire consequences.

As so often happens, encounters are linked to characters and I can still well remember many of those of my youth. One was an old inshore fisherman by the name of

Tim Holbrook, a rather aged gentleman who had spent his life earning, often a meagre living, by catching prawns, lobsters and crabs, working from a sixteen-foot rowing boat. No outboard motors in those days. During the season, herring would be netted and at a certain time of the year, and with a fair amount of luck, the more profitable red mullet would be caught. It was usually in September and during calm weather that a shoal of mullet would come close inshore and under such conditions, providing you were in the right position on the cliff top, a faint pink patch could be seen just below the surface of the sea. When a shoal was spotted there was a mad rush by the local "small boat" men to "shoot" a net which would ensure a good haul of this valuable fish. It was therefore the custom for the older, often partially retired men, to be on the cliffs looking out for the telltale pink hue.

On one particular afternoon, a couple of us lads were walking along the cliffs when we came upon the aforementioned Tim Holbrook, sitting on a seat with his eyes glued on the mirror-like sea. We knew him well and so we stopped for a chat, but never once did his gaze move from scanning the blue Solent. There were still the remnants of the summer visitors about and, as we were talking to him, two such "overners" (people visiting the island) came strolling along. They stopped to have a word with Tim and after a while, being rather curious as to why his gaze did not leave the sea, one said:

"What are you looking at my man?"

Whereupon Tim pointed to the distant horizon and replied: "I'm looking at that ship just out of sight."

The visitors departed rather nonplussed, no doubt thinking they had been talking to a bit of a nutcase! That was very far from the truth for they were hardly out of sight when Tim jumped up onto the seat for a better view and then, despite his age, dashed off with a good turn of speed. We took his place on the seat and awaited developments. Soon we could see two boats being rowed out from the shore and very soon the nets were going over the sterns, to encircle the shoal of mullet which by now had come close inshore on the flood-tide. We watched with great interest as the fishermen splashed the water with their oars as they drove the shoal of "pink beauties" to be enmeshed in the nets. In what seemed no time at all, the two boats were on their way back to the shore, so we made our way to meet them as they grounded in the shallow water. The boats, to our young eyes, seemed full of a pink and shimmering mass, for there was, without a doubt, a lot of fish in those two boats that afternoon.

I can still see the red mullet on my plate that tea-time, for we both were given a fish or two to take home. I suppose it could again be called a profitable encounter. It certainly was for the fisherman and, to a lesser degree, to ourselves.

Sadly, the red mullet is rarely seen in the Solent waters these days and even the humble herring is as scarce as the pound note on an offertory plate in pre-war days!

Without a doubt, Tim Holbrook was a great attraction for the summer visitors. In his later years, he spent many hours gazing out to sea, no doubt thinking about the adventures he must have had whilst fishing in those waters. Many liners would be passing down the Solent in those days, going to places on the other side of the world, and scores of merchant ships would be ploughing their way to the then great port of Southampton.

Once, during a spell of little activity on those busy waters, Tim was looking at a newspaper that he had probably picked up, more than likely to keep his "patch" tidy. He was sitting on his usual seat with his peaked "yachting" cap at an angle and despite it being a hot day, he was wearing a thick roll-neck woollen jersey. All these inshore fishermen wore such clothing and upon a close inspection it would be found that most of the jerseys had the name of a yacht "picked out". In those days the crew-men, even on a small yacht, wore woollen garments and their jerseys, embroidered with their vessel's name, would be handed down to the locals, hence the necessity of some needlework to remove the name.

Tim was sitting there enjoying the balmy breeze and occasionally a passer-by would have a few words with the old lad. A crowd of strangers approached and one or two paused to chat to the retired "sea dog". He was staring at his paper and one of the friendly strangers remarked: "You have the paper upside down, my fellow."

"Aye, I knows," says Tim. "Any damn fool can read it tother way up!"

Even so, it is more than likely that it wouldn't make any difference which way up the paper was, it being doubtful if he could read at all.

One more tale about that old fisherman friend of mine, for he was a friend, always having a chat and a cheerful word to us lads. This particular incident happened on the lane between Tim's house and the village shops. The old lad was on his way to get a supply of his favourite "weed" from the tobacconist, when he met a complete stranger. The smart looking gentleman stopped Tim to ask directions for a certain cottage.

"I wonder if you could tell me, my good man, if I am anywhere near Rose Cottage?"

"Certainly I can tell you, sir," Tim replied. "It be down this 'ere lane, best part of a mile, on the right hand side, you canna miss it. There's artificial roses growing round the front door." The stranger shouted his thanks but he couldn't see the grin on Tim's face for Rose Cottage was the old chap's abode! It was never discovered if the stranger called at the stone cottage, or if he ever knew that Tim Holbrook lived there.

Perhaps these encounters about Tim Holbrook don't amount to much, but they at least show that this particular fisherman had a fair turn of wit and, at the same time, an unusual knack of answering questions without answering them.

My grandfather and uncle were both inshore fishermen, operating from Bembridge, and as I was born in that same village and spent all my schooldays there, it was inevitable that I should often be out in boats. On one occasion, grandfather asked me to go with him and "shoot" his prawn pots. This entailed rowing out of the harbour for a couple of miles or so and then dropping the pots into fairly shallow water, adjacent to a certain type of sea grass or weed, the favourite haunt of that most tasty of the shrimp family, the prawn.

It was a question of very delicate timing, for at certain states of the tide it was almost impossible to row a boat, laden with four dozen prawn pots, against a strong current. It was always a case of rowing as there were few motors available for small boats in those days and doubtful if those fishermen could have afforded one anyway. No matter what time of day the right tide should be, that was the time to set off. The boat would be cast off from the mooring and out into the channel to get the benefit of the strong current and with a laden boat little rowing was needed to arrive at the selected spot to "shoot" the pots.

I well remember grandfather saying: "Be down at the harbour at ten to seven this evening and not a minute later; we'll be leaving at three minutes past."

Of course, I was there in plenty of time and we were soon being carried out of the harbour on the strong tide. At the harbour buoy, about a mile from land, grandfather started to really row and soon told me to get into the bow of the boat and tell him when I saw grass-like weed in the clear water.

"There's some, grandad," I soon shouted, whereupon he stopped rowing, looked over the side and then dropped a "pot" with its three stones tied to anchor it over the side. Thus we progressed, me spotting the weed, grandfather checking and then dropping a pot at the appropriate spot, not amongst the mass of green fronds, but on a sandy spot close by. When all the pots, with their smelly, salted herring bait had been put over the side, I looked back and could see a long line of bobbing pieces of cork on the calm water. The corks were fastened to rope attached to the pots so that they could

14

be hauled from the depths, with, hopefully, a good catch of prawns. Once all the pots were set, grandfather took out his pipe and, sitting in the stern of the boat, soon had a cloud of smoke rising in the air as if coal had been put on a boiler! Fire but no power in this sixteen foot "pot" boat, only human muscle.

After a while the old chap said: "We'll make our way back slowly," and thus he started to row back to the harbour entrance, but when we reached the harbour buoy, he rowed up to it and told me to tie the boat to one of the several rings on the side of this marker to the channel entrance. "We've been pretty quick today," he said. "It would be you spotting the right places for me to put a pot."

"Shall we have to stay here long?" I asked.

"No not long. Another twenty minutes or so, and there will be little strength in the out-going tide."

After another cloud of smoke had risen from the glowing pipe, we cast off to row home on the now slack tide. Once ashore, after tying up in the harbour, grandfather led me to the nearest hostel, a pub called the "Pilot Boat". I was not old enough to enter the portals, but grandad went in and shortly after came out with a glass of lemonade, yellow it was and tasted like real lemons (not like today's insipid stuff). Even as I write I can taste that drink which was pure nectar to me. Maybe it was the salt on my lips from the gentle sea breeze that made that drink taste so good, but it is certainly a drink that I have always remembered.

The next morning, at the right state of the tide, the old chap set off to haul his pots and take out the night's catch. Even with the number of pots each fisherman used, their catch would often be quite small, only a hundred or so prawns, barely earning a living for all that hard work. This particular morning my grandfather was in high glee for as he lifted each pot from the sea bed, it contained several handfuls of the almost transparent delicacy. As the pots were emptied they were rebaited and returned to the sandy bottom. Once the catch was in

15

the special basket in his boat, grandfather returned to the harbour as quickly as possible for there was work to be done.

As he walked up the hill to his cottage, he greeted the few people about at that early hour with a smile and a cheery "Good morning", for his spirits were high, the catch had been a good one. When he arrived at his house, grandmother had a large oval pan on the outhouse fire, with the water therein boiling gaily away.

All the prawns were emptied into the bubbling water and after a fixed amount of time, only minutes, the pan was removed from the heat and the water drained off. By now the prawns had changed colour from their normal translucent green to a lovely pale pink, a great big heap of them. The next part of the process, while the prawns were still warm, was to add salt. This was done by placing a quantity on a large plate, rather like an over-grown meat dish, and shaking them about until the salt disappeared. They were then emptied onto a large wooden perforated tray to allow them to cool. When all the prawns had been salted, grandfather sat down to a well-earned breakfast, followed by a peaceful pipe smoked, and then there was work to be done.

All the prawns had to be packed into small wooden boxes, similar to the wooden boxes used by gardeners for seed sowing. Each box held a given number, which of course had to be counted as the box was filled. Any small specimens were put on one side as the work proceeded. Once all the prawns had been packed and the wooden lids nailed down, labels were attached and the boxes loaded onto a wheelbarrow.

I remember the fishermen's wheelbarrows were side-less ones, though the reason escapes me. Down the hill to the railway station went grandfather with a full load and soon his prawns were on their way to London where the best prices could be obtained through the whole-salers. Speed was of the essence and those boxes of prawns would soon be in town for, even after crossing the Solent on the ferry, it was under a four-hour journey and

16

things ran to time in those days. London was a good market and fresh caught prawns were in great demand, so much so, that at that particular time, the price was around two pence per prawn, so even a catch of two hundred and fifty or so was most satisfactory, especially when considering that the average wage in those days was only about thirty shillings.

Grandfather had a real haul. The number of prawns he had boxed was three thousand and there were also a number of smaller specimens he could sell locally for a shilling a hundred.

Then there were the lobsters. My uncle, who had been an inshore fisherman all his life, called at my home one day and said, "Would you like to come with me this evening, I'm showing a gentleman how to catch lobster?" Naturally I jumped at the chance and was at the meeting place some while before the appointed time. After what seemed an age, I could see my uncle approaching, attired in his normal thigh boots, accompanied by a gentleman wearing shorts. Over my uncle's shoulder was a large crowbar and what appeared to be a length of very stout wire. This item had a short bend at one end and I was soon to discover to what use it would be put.

We went down onto the beach and headed for the ledges, making our way out to the furthest lagoon in which were a number of seaweed covered large rocks or boulders.

"That looks a likely one," said my uncle as we approached a particularly large specimen. By the time we got there, the water was well above my knees

My uncle looked around and lifted a large stone from beneath the water and placed it in position near to the boulder. On his instructions we positioned ourselves around the boulder under which uncle pushed the crowbar and proceeded to rock it, using the stone as a fulcrum. Nothing happened, so after a while he used the length of strong wire to rake under the boulder, as a housewife would use a scraper whilst cleaning out the flue. Again nothing, so we moved on to another similar boulder not far away. The process was repeated again without success, but my uncle was not deterred saying many factors could be involved, the wind, the tide and probably most important, the temperature of the water. However, he was sure he would be successful ere long.

Finally, we came across a smaller boulder which was almost submerged and was rather flattish, more so than the previous ones which we had tried without success. "Ah, this looks the best yet," said my uncle as he searched for a "fulcrum" stone. Soon the crowbar was under the rock and uncle was putting his weight on it to move the boulder, rocking it gently up and down. Nothing ! But then the wire with a crook went under, and whoosh, out shot a lobster.

"Grab him," shouted uncle, for it was heading my way. I made a lunge and missed it. Fortunately, I had turned it in uncle's direction and with what seemed no effort, he put his hand in the water and brought it out. A beauty, about a pound and a half and oh, what lovely colours.

Moving inland to another lagoon where the water was not quite so deep, several rocks were tried without success and it was almost time to retreat shoreward.

"Just one more," uncle remarked as the procedure started all over again. This time, however, on the first bit of pressure the rock toppled over and out shot what we had been searching for. It went close to uncle and he made an attempt to pluck it out of the water but without success. It turned and passed close to the gentleman who grabbed it with both hands and with a joyful shout, brought it out of the water. Uncle was now satisfied for it was certain he wanted this gentleman to actually catch a lobster himself, and looking back I am sure he missed it on purpose.

The gentleman was really pleased and could not stop looking at his prize as we walked up the beach. As we made our way into the village uncle said, "I'll cook both of them for you, sir, and you may have them for dinner tomorrow."

"That will be fine," the gentleman replied, "but why

don't you use one of those shrimp nets to lift them out of the sea? I'm sure it would be easier that way."

"Aye," agreed my uncle, "but you see, if everyone did that, lobsters would soon be scarce in those pools. As it is now, more escape than are caught."

As we parted the gentleman slipped a coin into my uncle's hand saying, "I'll pay you for the lobsters tomorrow."

"Thank you very much Mr Niven," my uncle replied.

Thus ended my encounter with Mr David Niven who, at that time, was virtually unknown, but later became a very famous film star.

As a lad, the most important things in my life were birds nesting, fishing and walking along the shore, but not necessarily in that order. Fishing from the shore on a baking summer's evening was a delight when the state of the tide was right. Bembridge Harbour has quite a narrow entrance and this was the favoured spot to fish. Using hand-lines baited with the usual ragworm, it was surprising how many we hauled ashore.

Two or three of us were waiting for the tide to recede, so that we could get to our favourite spot, and as it ebbed a large expanse of sand, like a finger of gold, could be seen running out to sea for almost a mile. Here and there were shallow pools, seldom more than a foot deep, and as the pools became isolated from the receding sea, crowds of seagulls would appear and swoop down on the placid pools. Much small marine life was reachable to the diving, wheeling gulls and even small fish, mostly plaice and flounders, would be eaten by the hungry hordes. These gulls were mostly herring gulls or black headed gulls, but as we watched, a larger, darker bird appeared out of the summer sky.

It was a black-backed gull, a larger cousin. As we watched it swooped a number of times and struck at the shallow water, but the distance prevented us from being able to see what was being taken. After a few minutes of such antics, we saw the gull struggle to rise from the water, but eventually it did so, only to be mobbed by many of the other gulls, a not uncommon occurrence. We quickly became aware that the black-headed gull had quite a large object suspended beneath it and we jumped, shouted and clapped our hands to make it drop the prize which was obviously a fish. The bird rose and fell in the air, wheeling and dodging his tormentors, but still clung tight to what he hoped would be a good feed. The longer the spectacle continued, the more we lads shouted and gesticulated. Probably exhaused from its efforts, the gull eventually came to land some hundred yards from where we stood and the gang of us made one mad rush towards it. The bird tried hard to rise again with its catch but as we got closer the approaching danger became too much and a large wriggling fish fell to the sand. It was a flat fish, a beautiful specimen of plaice, with lovely orange-like circles on its upper side.

We did eventually start fishing, but everything we caught that evening was over-shadowed by the antics of the aerial fisherman. When we got home and weighed it, the fish topped the scales at just short of one pound four ounces. We never were sure whether the gull was a Lesser or Greater Blackbacked, such finer points being lost in the excitement. Its size certainly gave the impression that it was a Greater Blackbacked of which there were quite a number to be seen on the mudflats at low water.

Fishing was our main pastime during the summer holidays, although our tackle was rather basic to say the least. A good, stout line, often wound round a piece of driftwood, a medium sized pebble with a hole in it for a weight, "lucky stones" we called them, and with a couple of hooks on short lengths of line attached just above the weight, our fishing gear was complete. A garden fork between five or six lads was also needed to dig for the bait.

It was a typical summer evening as we set off. It had been a hot day although the balmy onshore breeze was beginning to increase in strength, rippling the incoming tide into wavelets. However, this didn't deter us from our purpose. One of the lads had been digging bait before the morning high tide and the wooden bait box was writhing with big flat worms, both "lob and wrag". It was not long before the handlines were sailing out into the channel, carried by the weight of the lucky stones. The tide was well on the turn and flowing strongly into the harbour. This was often a profitable time for fishing and proved so this evening, for every line was bringing in nice sizeable "flatties" (we always returned the small ones) and, of course, a few "king crabs". These we detested because they ate the bait and were nothing but a nuisance.

The tide continued to rise and as it did so, the wind increased making the earlier wavelets into waves eighteen inches high which broke on the sand and washed around our legs. Several of the lads were ready to retreat with their bag of flatties, but I insisted on one more cast. "Only a couple of minutes," said one of the gang. "If we don't go soon this wind will push the sea across the sand flats and cut us off."

I was just about to haul in my line when I felt an almighty tug and I knew at once that a fish of some size was pulling at the other end. The line went out seawards and then came back with a rush up the channel on the tide and though it seemed ages, I could eventually see what appeared a gigantic shape weaving about below the surface and ocasionally breaking through the waves. There was much excitement amongst the gang, for such a size fish on a handline had not been hooked before and as the fish gradually tired we knew it was a bass and a fine specimen at that.

As I pulled the silver fish out on to the sand, it shook and flapped in the unfamiliar element, but as it quietened down, I made to get hold of it to remove the hook. Just as I touched it, there was one great flap and as the fish turned over one of the sharp spines on the dorsal fin entered my finger underneath a nail. Not another thought was given to that as with the hook removed we stepped out quickly to reach the shore before the incoming tide cut us off. What a fish that bass was.

When weighed in it topped the scales at over nine pounds and was the talk amongst the local lads for the rest of the fishing season.

There was an outcome to this encounter which I personally shall never forget. A few days after landing the bass my finger had swollen to the size of two and the pain was almost unbearable. At night the intense agony prevented me from sleeping and my mother was getting concerned that the poison might spread. The flesh beneath the nail had turned a muddy yellow and the throbbing seemed to keep time with the ticking of the clock. On the fourth night as I lay moaning in bed, mother appeared carrying a large bowl of hot, almost boiling water, which she used to bathe the infected finger. At first this seemed to increase the agony but as the water cooled, so did the intensity of the pain. What a relief!

I missed many fishing evenings in the channel that summer although I used to be with the lads as they hauled in their lines, getting their usual catch of flounder and plaice. Seventy years later, I still have a misshapen finger-nail as a permanent reminder of that nine pound bass.

Keepers and Dogs

S chooldays inevitably came to an end and the pranks had to come to an end as well. The time had arrived to look for gainful employment. In those days, shortly after the General Strike, it was not easy to find a job. Some lads went as labourers, the odd one was lucky enough to get an apprenticeship, another was employed as a van lad, helping with general carriage and local deliveries, although in the end he did run his own business.

The problem of my future was eventually solved by what was really a chance encounter. At that time my father was Chief Steward on a yacht, the "Cutty Sark", owned by the Second Duke of Westminster. She was lying in Southampton water and my father arranged for my mother, my brother and myself to travel to Southampton and spend the day looking over the vessel.

It was a lovely summer day and the trip down Southampton Water in a fast launch was exhilarating. It was travelling so fast, that sitting at the stern, it appeared as if you were below the level of the sea. Once on board the yacht, it was another world.

Everything was perfect. All the brasswork shone and only the port holes made you realise that you were on a yacht and not in a large house, or so it seemed to my youthful eyes. After a conducted tour of the whole yacht, from the engine room to the galley and the bridge, we had lunch in the crew's dining room. Shortly afterwards, the Chief Officer appeared and announced that the launch had left the yacht and was on its way to bring the

Duke aboard. It was a completely unexpected visit as he was not scheduled to leave for France until two days later. Our family were aboard and we had no option but to stay there until the launch returned when father said we would be taken back to Southampton. The Duke duly arrived and we were preparing to go down the gangplank onto the launch to start our journey back home. As we appeared on deck, the Duke also came into view from the direction of the stern of the ship. He approached us and said how pleased he was to see the family on board and hoped we had enjoyed the "inspection", as he called it. He then enquired, knowing the family tradition, if I was going to sea. Father explained that as I suffered from bronchitis it was unlikely, but hopefully something would turn up.

"It has turned up now," said the Duke. "If the lad is prepared to go to my country seat, Eaton Hall, I will instruct my agent, Major Basil Kerr, to find a job for him."

He then asked me what I was interested in and, I suppose being taken rather by surprise, I replied, "Wildlife, sir."

"Ah very good," said the Duke. "You can join the game department at Eaton. I have a very good headkeeper, a Mr Stark. You will be under him."

With that he left us and we went ashore in the launch. Father, of course, had to go back aboard as the "Cutty Sark" was to sail that evening, bound for Deauville, in France.

Within a week, a letter arrived from Major Kerr, instructing that I could take up my post at Eaton whenever it was suitable and that lodgings were being arranged.

Eventually, I arrived at Eaton, on October 9th, 1929, and I was to complete fifty years service in the employ of the Grosvenor family, working for four Dukes of Westminster. That chance meeting with the Second Duke on the "Cutty Sark" was certainly a most fortunate one for me and getting to Eaton was an encounter in itself.

The journey entailed a day's travelling via the mainland ferry and then a long train journey which involved crossing London. I had never been on a journey of any description, so the travelling was certainly an unforgettable adventure. Fortunately, my parents were with me, or else otherwise I would, undoubtedly, have got lost.

The speed of the train, from Portsmouth to London, seemed amazing, at any rate to me who had only previously travelled on slow-stopping trains, and then only for eight or ten miles or so. Arriving in London, there was a choice of crossing to Euston Station, either by underground or by taxi. As there were several large cases, a taxi was called and the trip across the big city began. This was another encounter with something new, for even in those far off days the traffic seemed tremendous, but then I suppose a mere trickle compared with today. To me then they were travelling at such a speed that crashes seemed inevitable.

After much whistle-blowing and shouting at Euston Station, our train started to pull out and soon the buildings and houses were beginning to flash past, although it seemed ages before this kaleidoscope of bricks and mortar gave way to open country.

The clickety, clickey, click of the train's wheels changed their note as the train roared through the wayside stations, pressing on ever further northwards, just one stop, Rugby, before we had to change at Crewe. The half-hour run to Chester was in darkness and only the twinkling lights of the farms and cottages could be seen. There was just one stop, at Beeston Castle, but no-one alighted or boarded the train. Years later, I learned that all trains had to stop here because of an agreement between the landowner and the railway company when the route from Crewe to Chester was being laid.

It was early evening when we arrived in Chester, but too late to travel out to Eaton Hall, so a taxi took us to the Stafford Hotel, in City Road. After we had settled in, there was an evening to pass and father and mother decided it would be pleasant to spend it at the local theatre. I remember it was a variety programme, much like the old-time "music hall". Looking back, I suppose it was the old-time music hall ! Up to then the occasional visit to a cinema had been my only experience of "provided" entertainment.

The next morning, after a hearty breakfast, a taxi was called to take us out to the Duke of Westminster's Estate, a distance of about five miles. The route was through the centre of Chester, which at that time of the morning was alive with shoppers and, here and there, horses, carts, traps and floats. Sometimes there would be a man holding a horse whilst its owner went about his business. This was a source of income for some of the unemployed of the city, for even a few coppers could mount up in the course of a day, especially when the market was taking place.

As we approached the outskirts of the city, the Grosvenor Bridge came into view and soon we were in the suburb of Chester known as Handbridge, part of the Duke's Estate. From here it was a nice run mainly through farmland and with occasional glimpses of the River Dee. After about two miles, we came to a small village which our friendly taxi driver told us was called Eccleston. All the cottages, substantially built and well spaced, were occupied by Estate workers, a model village, in fact, with its church and post office, but no pub, though there had once been one.

Not far out of the village was the entrance to the large park and as we approached the ornate wrought-iron gates, we were met by the lodgekeeper, upright and dressed in frock coat and top hat, with cockade. He was attired in what I was later to learn was the Westminter livery of dark blue with gold piping, which was also the Duke's racing colours.

Eaton Hall, my first encounter with a "stately home", was a massive building even viewed from the trades-men's entrance but, fortunately, father knew some of the household staff who had been on the Duke's yacht at various times. We were soon settled in the servants' hall where morning coffee and biscuits were brought to us. It seemed strange to be waited on in a large room in a stately home. I learned later that the staff was so large that servants were employed to wait on the servants.

At exactly two o'clock, the man in charge of the game department put in an appearance. He was a fine figure of a man, dressed in a tweed suit of plus fours, or more accurately plus twos, with what I would call a well trimmed "goatee" beard, and with a tremendous smile which was extenuated by his ruddy cheeks. Here was truly the face of a man who spent all his life in the open air.

"My name's Stark, Head Keeper," he announced. "This is the lad joining our department, I assume?"

After chatting with us for a while, we set off for my lodgings. Whilst we had been in the servants' hall, there had been a skittering of snow and in the afternoon sun the overhanging branches and shrubs were a wonderful sight as we drove down one of the Estate drives. After travelling for about three miles there came into view another set of large wrought-iron gates that extended the full width of the drive. In those days this was the drive used by the Duke when attending Chester Races and other important events in the city; the rest of the time the gates were kept closed. I was to lodge with the lodgekeeper, a single man whose sister kept house for him. Out of my £4 per month wages I was to pay board of fifteen shillings a week, leaving me five bob... not much by today's standards, but reasonable then.

And so began my fifty years on the Duke of Westminster's Estate.

My first instruction was to meet up with a party of gamekeepers and woodmen for the purpose of driving pheasants back to their home coverts. At the same time, rabbits, hares, woodcock and maybe pigeon were to be shot, to stock up the larder at Eaton Hall.

Mr Stark introduced me to all of the gamekeepers present, five or six if memory serves me rightly. There were twenty keepers on the Estate, but it was rare for them all to be in one place, except on shooting days. I joined in with the party as they drove the driveside woods back towards the Hall some two miles away. I was amazed at the number of pheasants and rabbits that were about and now and again a keeper would have a shot at a pheasant or other target, but only a pheasant flying back the way we had come. Every so often there were openings in the woods and when we came to these, a halt was called and any rabbits or pheasants that had been shot were taken and put in the attending "float". This vehicle was pulled by a horse in the charge of one of Stark's lads. A halt to the day's driving was finally called, close to one of the keepers' cottages. The keeper who lived there came to me and said, "You'd better come for a cup of tea lad, it's a long walk back you have."

He was right and I was sure glad of that cup of tea for night was falling by the time I had walked almost three miles back to my lodgings.

The shooting season for game birds had already begun, but it was usual for the Second Duke to wait until the end of November before any large shoots were organised, for by then the birds were mature and not only stronger flyers, but also a better size for the table. Many preparations had to be made before a large shoot could take place, not least of which was ensuring that the bulk of the pheasants that were going to be shot were in the woods.

The Hall was virtually in the centre of the Estate and the driveways, like the spokes in a wheel, radiated in all directions, no doubt to facilitate the travel arrangements in the days of the carriage, rather than the motor car.

One drive, as already mentioned, led to Chester with a second running almost parallel. Another wended its way towards the North Wales coast after a dead straight mile and three quarters and then a couple of miles through well-wooded country. Another also led into North Wales, but this one finished at Broughton Church. A fifth and shorter carriageway came out at Aldford village, a part of the Estate which was the site of the Home Farm and, at one time, the Stud Farms.

These produced all the horses needed to run a large Estate but, regrettably some might may say, they have now been replaced by tractors and the like. The sixth and final drive branched off the main Aldford drive, after it had crossed the River Dee, and came out on the main trunk road between Chester and Whitchurch. This was the drive to Crewe and the main-line trains to London.

The total length of these drives is somewhere around fifteen miles.

During those early days on the Estate, I had my first encounter with a fox when one jumped out of a thick bramble bush whilst we were driving the driveside woods one morning. I had never seen a live fox before and it took me completely by surprise.

It was a large animal and, when disturbed, displaced quite an area of the bramble patch with the "ripples" travelling some distance. Then a rich reddish brown form appeared and headed across an opening, making for the nearest cover, a large patch of privet bushes. A lovely sight, I suppose, but I did not readily have time to appreciate it for it was only a matter of seconds before Reynard was out of sight. I half expected to hear a shot from the keepers standing across the wood several hundred yards ahead, but no, not a sound. Later, I was to be told that the keepers were under orders not to shoot foxes for they were needed for the hunt. There were many more encounters with foxes over the years and not all of them were as lucky.

Life as a teenager, and the sights and sounds, were much different on a large estate than in a small village on the Isle of Wight. For a start, the people here spoke, what seemed to me at first, a foreign language, although in due course I got used to the Cheshire dialect. Then there were the different birds, the sea fishing species being replaced by the fresh water variety on the River Dee and the numerous ponds, or marl pits, that dot the Cheshire plain. No longer could I listen to the waves beating on the shore when the wind was strong, nor hear the foghorns of the liners and cargo vessels passing through the Solent. There were no white, or red, sails to be seen gliding across the water on a steady breeze and the fishermen in navy blue jerseys were replaced by gamekeepers in dark grey, heavy duty tweeds, "pepper and salt" was the term they used to describe the colour.

On most working days, when getting the pheasants together, the keepers would be in these "pepper and salt" suits which were really of white and black material, so giving a dark grey appearance.

I reckon the white represented the salt, but the "pepper" must have been of the black variety.

Most of the men also wore "box cloth" leggings for the nether garments were breeches and the leggings gave good protection from the brambles and other rough herbage that was part of the daily trudging. It was quite an encounter to see eight or ten such men dressed, more or less, like peas in a pod, with the occasional difference in headgear, although most wore trilby hats.

If everyone was carrying a gun, it almost gave the impression of a small platoon from a private army. Maybe on thinking about it, that is what they were, since their main task for a large part of the year was to protect the game on the Estate. I suppose way back in history, similar men also had to protect their Lord and Master.

On shooting days there was a dramatic change. At Eaton all the gamekeepers had a "velvet" livery which had to be worn when His Grace was entertaining guests on a day's shoot. This regalia was really something.

The jackets were of green velvet, as were the waistcoats, each article having brass buttons with the Grosvenor Crest embossed upon them, and of course these buttons had to really shine. The breeches were, of all things, made in a white cord, but each keeper did have two pairs for after washing, and that was needed after only one day's wear, they took some drying. Box cloth leggings were again worn, but these had to have been freshly scrubbed and naturally the boots were of stout leather and highly polished, up to army standard. Brown footwear was not allowed as the wearer would have stood out and that would not do.

A white shirt with a stiff white collar was also an integral part of the livery and only a black tie would serve around the neck. Headgear on these occasions was changed from workaday wear to a blocker, otherwise known as a "hard hat". These hats were adorned with gold braid with a bow in the front and the senior keepers had a larger amount of braid than the juniors.

It seemed to be the rule that the sticks the keepers carried were all of the same style. The Scottish name for this particular style is "ol crummock".

This straight stick, cut to length to suit the user, had a "vee" at the end in which the thumb rested whilst walking. In many areas this is normally called a "thumb stick". As quite a number of gamekeepers in those days were Scotsmen, the Scottish name for this particular style of walking aid seemed to be in common use.

Large estates were much different then and many men and women were employed in the various departments. Each department had its own "head" and the staff were required to maintain in perfect condition what could be a very large area indeed.

The Hall itself had a vast number of servants with a House Steward in command, whilst outdoors, the Head Gardener was responsible for the gardens and glass houses. It was the Clerk of Works who had to ensure all the buildings, cottages and farms, were kept in tip-top condition, whilst the Farm Manager was in charge at the Home Farm. The Head Forester looked after the extensive woodlands and the environment generally, including main water courses, brooks and ditches and drive verges.

The Head Keeper, with many keepers under his command, was responsible for all the sporting activities. Gamekeepers were classed as "outdoor domestic servants", being, in effect, directly responsible to the Duke. In between all departments and the Duke was the

Estate Agent. This gentleman, for most of them in pre-war days were men of means, dealt with the overall running of the Estate, normally through regular meetings with the heads of departments.

As a lad who had never seen, yet alone been involved with a large estate or a big shoot, it was all an encounter with new faces and new situations, though as the weeks went by it quickly became a normal way of life, with much of interest to be seen and heard.

Certainly, one of the most fascinating jobs was ferreting for rabbits. In fact, I had never even seen a ferret before, let alone handled one. It came about that a number of rabbits were needed in the Hall kitchens as, apparently, it was the custom that "Game Pie" was always available. The recipe called for rabbit meat and as the pies were quite large, a number of rabbits. Pheasants and hares also had to be provided by the keepers. Thus, I was detailed to report to accompany one of the keepers to catch the required number of rabbits. The first task was to get the ferrets out of their quarters, but the keeper wouldn't let me pick them up at that stage, "They know me," he said. "If you try to pick them up, they may give you a nip."

I had already seen their sharp teeth and I certainly didn't want that. My mentor put three of the ferrets into a box with a strap attached and then we went into a building which had several benches, tools hanging from the walls, and a wash boiler on one side. There was also a smell of what seemed like a mixture of gun oil and porridge oats.

The ferret box was placed on one of these benches and a ball of string taken from a drawer. I wondered what the string was for and I was soon to find out. Half a dozen pieces were cut, each about fifteen inches long, and two were taken up and deftly tied together, thus making three double pieces of string. Now the keeper took one of the ferrets from the box and handed it to me, with the remark, "Don't hold it too tight and you'll be alright."

As he then picked up one of the double pieces of string

he said, "Now if you put your thumb on the animal's head and a finger under its jaw, it will open its mouth."

What the deuce for, I wondered, but did as I was instructed. Sure enough the mouth came open and as it did so the keeper put the string over the bottom jaw. With deft movements he soon tied the string in two places. When all three had been tied up in this manner, I was told, "There, they can't bite you now, and they won't be able to bite a rabbit either, but they should make 'im bolt."

After gathering a game bag of small nets, purse nets I was told, and a narrow-bladed spade we went out into the woods.

"We're looking for small rabbit burrows," the keeper said. "We don't want to dig if we can help it, but the rabbits should bolt alright today."

Of course, he knew where all the burrows were on his patch and we soon came upon a suitable one. "Now no talking," I was told as we approached up wind. Next the purse nets were spread out over the rabbit holes and pegged down securely by applying pressure to the wooden pegs with the heel of a boot. All the holes were then covered, making very sure that none had been missed, including those that appeared to be merely depressions in the ground filled with leaves but, as I was later to learn, were escape routes for the rabbits. Two ferrets which we had muzzled earlier were taken from the carrying box and slipped quietly through the nets, one through a net over what seemed to be a well used hole and the other one onto a hole partly full of leaves.

Standing fairly close, but still downwind from the nets, it was a matter of waiting patiently for the ferrets to do their job. Suddenly, there was a rushing sound and a shower of leaves from a little-used hole as a rabbit burst out into daylight and into the purse net. The keeper took a couple of quick strides, grabbed the net and at the same time put his foot over the hole from which the rabbit had bolted. In a few seconds the rabbit had been taken from the net and quickly dispatched.

The keeper then put the net back over the bolt hole and stood back to wait for another coney to appear. It was not a long wait as out jumped another bundle of fur and the earlier process was repeated.

Six or seven rabbits bolted from this small burrow before the ferrets emerged and they were quickly retrieved and placed back in the box.

The keeper told me in a quiet voice, for keepers do not talk loudly when in the woods, that I would now know why the nets were called purse nets, for they just pulled up tight when a rabbit entered, working with the same action as that of an old-fashioned purse, or "poke" as they were sometimes called.

He then slowly demonstrated to me how to set a net over an entrance to a burrow. At the next small burrow, it wasn't long before a coney appeared and as as the keeper gathered up rabbit and net, I quickly set a replacement. We soon had fourteen rabbits, although the keeper said that only ten were wanted in the kitchen.

Next I was shown how to leg the rabbits, a simple process when you know how. All that needs to be done is to make a slit at the point between the back leg bone and the very strong sinew and then pass the other leg through the opening created. This can be done quickly and easily with a bit of practice and the use of a very sharp knife normally carried by all keepers. Once legged, the rabbits were strung on a short length of stout cord which the keeper produced from his spacious pocket. Swinging the rabbits over his shoulder, he left me to carry back to his cottage the ferret box, the bag of nets and the unused spade. The ferrets were put back into their hutch after removing the muzzles and, because it had been a dry day and there was no need to dry them, the purse nets were returned to the proper place.

"Now we have to belly the rabbits," said the keeper as he proceeded to show me what to do. Holding the rabbit almost around the middle, behind the front legs with the head uppermost, he carefully made a small slit in the belly of the coney. Placing the knife between the fingers of the hand holding the rabbit's neck, he used one finger of that hand and a finger of the free hand, to greatly enlarge the small slit. With this action, the bulk of the guts fell out and it was then very easy for these to be removed, ensuring that the bladder was taken away as well. Thus "paunched", the correct term for this process, the rabbits were hung up to set.

Later on, when recalling a poaching incident or two, I shall endeavour to describe another method used to take rabbits, a favourite method of poachers in those days, but also one employed by keepers and farmers. Instead of purse nets, a long net was used.

Ferreting reminds me of Sam, a black, curly-coated retriever that I once had. He was a large animal, not easy to control, but a very loyal dog.

I was due to meet my colleagues as we were to go ferreting and it was my turn to take the ferrets. We all had ferrets, but as we were after rabbits practically every day, we took it in turns to bring a box full of the lively little animals. I kept my ferrets in a large deer-shed about a mile from my home and as we were likely to be out most of the day, it was customary to take some sandwiches for our lunch.

As usual, I strapped my gun to the crossbar of my bike and went to loose Sam. As I moved away from the bike, Mrs Morgan, with whom I was lodging at the time, called from the house, "Don't forget your sandwiches," and she came to meet me with the parcel. I then put the packet of food down on a bench as I went to let Sam out of his kennel where he was jumping up and down with excitement. Later, upon arriving at the deershed, I put Sam to sit and went inside to select the ferrets for the day's work, putting four "gills" (females) in the carrying box. I then selected a large "fitchet", hob ferret, in case we had to use a line to dig a "laid up" gill out. Going back to my bike where Sam was sitting, I went over in my mind if I had all that was needed for the day.

A spade? Oh yes, Fred's bringing a spade so that's alright. Then thinking of what time we were likely to finish, sandwiches - where are they? Not in my pockets for sure, so did I pick them up off the bench ? "Damn," I said aloud and Sam looked up at me as much as to say "What's the matter ?"

"We'll have to go back, Sam. I've left the butties."

Sam stood up wagged his tail and without more ado was gone. I whistled and shouted as he got further away but only once did he stop and look back before he was off again. There was nothing I could do as he disappeared across the park, so I sat on some rails, lit my pipe and waited. I guessed he wouldn't be away long and if his destination, as it appeared, was back to my lodgings, his long legs would soon cover the best part of a mile.

It didn't seem very long before I heard a carrion crow with its "kronk kronk" mobbing something in the distance, and then I could just make out a small moving object at the far end of the park. Soon I could see it was Sam making a beeline for where he had left me and in his mouth was my packet of sandwiches!

He brought them straight to me with his tail going fifteen to the dozen and as I took the packet from him the paper was not even damp. He had a fine fuss made of him I can tell you. When I met the "gang" I related this story, but they didn't believe me though Sam kept looking at me and if he could have spoken I am sure he would have told the lads of what he had done. We had a good day's ferreting, the rabbits bolted well, and when we stopped for a snack those sandwiches tasted extra good. Perhaps it was the thought that many a dog would not have gone to get them or, at the very least, would have eaten them or mauled them on the way.

A toasted cheese butty does take some beating when

you are hungry and out in the fresh air. We used to light a small fire with dry twigs and when the smoke subsided, a sandwich was held over the heal on a forked stick and it was soon toasted and the cheese melted, lovely grub! I should say perhaps it was local made farm-house Cheshire cheese, the likes of which I find impossible to get today.

Over the years I had quite a number of dogs, springer spaniels, black labradors, golden labradors, flat-coated retrievers, and like Sam, a curly-coated retriever or two. This story is about a black labrador, not one of mine I must hasten to add, but one owned by another game-keeper. I can't really call this an encounter for I had known this particular dog since it was a pup, but I suppose I can say it was an encounter with grouse, those indigenous game birds of the heather.

Soon after the opening of the grouse shooting season, August 12th, my employer was holding a day's shooting on the moors in North Wales where the grouse were much more plentiful than they are today. Just ahead of us could be seen the "butts", man-made roofless shelters is probably the best way to describe them. They stretched for some distance along the shallow depression which was the end of the valley we had trudged up. The butts were probably seventy yards apart and that was where the gentlemen who were shooting were going to stand. Each butt was large enough for a "gun" whilst his loader and dog man would be out of sight of the grouse that would soon be driven towards them. Once all those concerned were out of sight in the butts, a signal was given, and in no time, coveys of grouse could be seen approaching. They were a long way away and most of them settled in the heather several hundred yards in front of the guns. As the beaters got nearer, the grouse started to get up and fly over the guns.

The shooting started and for a while there was quite a barrage, each gentleman getting through a considerable number of cartridges. After so much shooting there were many grouse to pick up and the dogs were soon busy.

The gentleman in the one butt had birds down behind him and I went to assist his dogman in the task.

The gun called to his man and said, "There is one wounded bird over there," pointing as he spoke to a large patch of moor, bare rock in fact, some hundred yards away.

"I'll send Tom," said the keeper, and the black labrador went. After about thirty yards he put his nose down and set off at great haste, obviously on the scent of a wounded bird. At somewhere close to the bare area, a grouse jumped up and Tom soon caught the bird and turned to return to the keeper with his trophy. At the point where he first put his nose down, Tom stopped and putting his head up in the air he placed the wounded bird on top of a high patch of heather, jumped a yard and picked up an obviously dead grouse. As he made a dash to his master with the second bird, I watched the first one flapping frantically on top of the heather. As I was on the point of sending my own dog, I caught sight of Tom heading back to the struggling bird which he was soon bringing back in his mouth.

Now after these two stories, one has to ask whether the actions of the two dogs involved was due to intelligence? There are mixed opinions on such matters. Many argue that so much that a dog does can be put down to routine, some say it is a natural instinct, whilst others, myself included, prefer to keep an open mind.

On shooting days, large numbers of people were involved, not the least of which were the beaters. Anything up to eighty would be needed to drive the pheasants over the guns out of the vast woodlands and once again a special dress was involved. Most of the men roped in for beating duties were employed on the Estate, in one department or another. The majority were foresters, or woodmen, as was the term in those days, whilst others would come from the garden staff and, of course, there were workers from the Home Farm and the Clerk of Works' department. All these men had to be dressed the same and it was truly a striking picture.

Starting with the headgear which was, what I can only describe as a bush hat, most eye-catching in a rich red. The hat had a leather band with a brass buckle, both of which had to really shine and when cocked up on the left side, reminded one of African style (except for the colour). Most of the beaters wore their normal working clothes, but these were enshrouded in a white smock. The smock was made of material almost like canvas, very thick, practically waterproof and impregnable, to all but the strongest thorn, and with this garment was worn a wide brown leather belt, again with a brass buckle and that essential shine. Brown, highly polished, leather leggings completed the dress though the footwear was non-descript, ranging from the odd shiny black pair of boots to heavily dubbined clogs. By and large such a rig-out gave good protection from both the weather and the hazards of the woods, for with the smock reaching below the knees, there was but little exposed.

With all these men being employed on the Estate, it was easy to ensure that the dress was uniform and woe betide any man or lad who appeared without being well turned out for it was not unknown for the headkeeper to inspect them at the start of the day. On one occasion he told a young lad, whose accoutrements were not as required, that he would give his mother a tin of boot polish if she didn't have any.

Others were involved when a large shoot was taking place, each guest requiring a man to load his guns and a lad to carry the cartridges and other equipment. This was looked upon as a choice job and usually undertaken by the tenant farmers and their sons, and generation followed generation. Once again dress came into it, not any uniformity in this case, but nevertheless there was some semblance in that direction, for it was the custom for the farmers to wear their "dressed up" clothes, those in which they would normally attend the local markets. These were highly polished boots, either black or brown, black or brown leather leggings, sometimes even brown leggings over black boots and almost all wore riding breeches, of course of different hues. A hacking jacket and a trilby hat completed the dress and it all was most suitable for the job in hand.

Of course, the Duke's guests included many well known gentlemen of that time, such as Mr Winston Churchill, later to become Sir Winston, and little did one think in 1929 that in little more than a decade he would be the saviour of our country. I shall always remember him as I saw him that day, resplendent in plus-fours and with a huge cigar jutting from his rugged features, nay "bulldog" like features, and he was an excellent shot. I did learn afterwards that on this particular day he was really in form for, according to an estate farmer, a certain Heber Fearnall, who had loaded his guns for him on numerous occasions, there were days when he could not hit the proverbial-haystack!

Mr Churchill used to come to almost every shooting day and once, when he shot a particularly high pheasant, the Duke told me to get the bird and put the tail feather in Winnie's hat. I stood there for a while and eventually plucked up courage; the would-be wartime leader just smiled and said: "You do that then, Lad".

During the war, I was on parade for an inspection by Churchill and as he walked down the line, he stopped, turned back, looked me in the face and said: "You're the man that stuck a feather in my cap." What an amazing memory!

Dogs are of course an integral part of a day's shooting and I was greatly impressed with my first encounter with the "dog men". Each of the Duke's guests had a "dog man" in attendance, whose duty was to retrieve any bird which had been hit but had travelled some distance afterwards. The men and dogs therefore were stationed some distance behind each gentleman who was shooting, at least a hundred yards behind, and under some circumstances, quite a bit more. Many of the men with dogs were gamekeepers from adjacent estates, well used to being able to tell if a pheasant had been wounded by the gentleman shooting. Any such birds were "marked" down and a dog sent to retrieve. Most of the dogs used were Labrador Retrievers, an odd Golden Retriever and now and again a Springer Spaniel, but they all did the same job, brought the marked bird back to the handler.

The very task that these keepers were performing meant they were mainly out of sight whilst the shooting was progressing and they only gathered together during the break for lunch. I did not see any of these keepers at their task until after lunch when two of them were standing a long way behind the guns, but out on an open field. My attention was riveted on one of them when I watched a pheasant that seemed to have been hit, "tower" at least a hundred and fifty yards from where the "gun" was standing. The bird had hardly hit the ground before a black labrador was sent to retrieve it, quite a simple retrieve no doubt, but I was really impressed with the speed with which that wounded bird was recovered. Perhaps wounded is not quite the right word for this particular incident, for when a game bird has been shot at and "towers" it usually means when it hits the ground it is already dead. "Tower" is the term used when a bird may be flying quite normally, then suddenly flies almost vertically with wings flapping frantically and then, suddenly, the flapping stops and the bird falls, usually dead. Here I must say that the main purpose of these dog men was to ensure that few, if any, wounded birds, were left to suffer. With each gentleman having a dog handler detailed to gather any wounded birds it was seldom that any were left until after nightfall, to be taken by a hungry fox.

I must not forget the cart that was in attendance to carry the game as it was gathered. Seeing the game-cart for the first time was in itself an encounter. A splendid sight, it was a four-wheeled, open vehicle drawn by one massive horse bedecked out with cockades. The cart was constructed to a special design, being built on what was basically a lorry with a curved roof about four feet high and in between there was a series of bars, each equipped with a large number of hooks on which the game could be hung. Each rail had a given number of hooks, so that things were made easy for the waggoner and his assistant to count the number of game on the cart. At the end of the day, there would be more than one thousand pheasants on the hooks and ready for the game larder.

They had to be hung in the game larder in the proper manner, not just haphazard, and that meant alternately, cock and hen. The hen pheasant has little colouring, but the cock bird is brilliant and with the long tails hanging down and overlapping the birds on the row beneath, it made a truly remarkable sight in the electric lights. I had never seen anything like it and yet there is a vague memory of a picture in a daily paper showing a shop full of Christmas fayre with all the future dinners hanging on high, but I fancy that they were mostly turkeys and chickens.

Woods and Foresters

The Head Forester and his team looked after the woods and coverts. There might be a large patch of briars that had taken over part of a wood and was holding up birds on a shooting day, or a belt of trees might be planted to improve the shooting at some spot. It was on one such planting project that I had my first encounter with the Head Forester, who was a Scotsman.

I was watching amazed at the speed young saplings were going in and it all seemed so easy. One man was using the spade and another was carrying a bundle of quite large saplings. There were also two more men working on the same line which consisted of a number of "sticks" lined up across the area to be planted. If I remember correctly, they started down a row and one pair would plant six young trees, two strides (about six feet I suppose) apart, and then the other pair took over and did the same, but the trees were different types, one oak and the other larch, a hardwood then a softwood. The man with the spade would cut a "T" in the ground, levering the soil up in the cross of the "T", whilst his partner pushed the young tree through the gap and then placed his foot firmly on the disturbed soil and moved on to the next. In no time at all they had covered the length of the plantation and then on turning round, ensured that the hardwood oak would be opposite the softwood larch. The next row they planted was of ash and Norway spruce. It thus became apparent that in due course, the wood, when eventually thinned, would be of a mixed nature. Suddenly, who should appear but the Head

Forester and for some reason, unknown to me at the time, the rapid progress in planting seemed to slow, whereas I had expected it to speed up. The Head Forester enquired how the job was going.

"Very well sir," replied one as he continued his labours.

The Head Forester then turned to me and said, "Come with me lad."

As he moved into the already planted area he stopped and tugged at one of the planted saplings which was quite firm. He then moved along the row trying each plant. Soon he came across a loose tree or two which came out of the ground as he pulled. After removing a number of the saplings he called one of the woodmen to him and said, "Do you think you have planted these trees?".

"Yes sir," came the reply.

"Well you can go along and plant them again. In fact, you can go down every row and stamp each sapling in firmly - all of you."

So the men had no option but to set off and do as instructed.

"There," said the head man, "You've learnt something. The men are on piece work at so much a hundred planted. They tend to rush the job to earn more, so checks have to be made."

On another occasion, a new plantation was laid out and was being planted purely as a game covert, so I was particularly interested in the procedure. It was to cover around four acres and was sited on high ground, but within a reasonable distance of established woods. This particular site seemed ideal to make it possible to present high flying pheasants as the guns would be able to stand at the lowest point between woods.

It had been decided to plant quite large quick-growing shrubs. This planting would enable pheasant poults to be put into the new plantation and eventually, before they reached maturity, they would roost in the adjacent mature covers. With this plan in mind, the woodmen had

44

already erected six-foot wire netting, within a post and rail fence, to keep out cattle. The wire netting had small mesh at the bottom and larger on top, the small mesh to keep the numerous rabbits and hares out. It would also ensure that any pheasants released in the new plantation would be reasonably secure from foxes until such time as they went to roost.

As the woodmen were busy planting, I was standing outside the wire perimeter, trying to determine the area which would eventually be all shrubs and, obviously, the point from which, on a shooting day, the pheasants would be flushed.

As I stood surveying the scene, I could also hear the "pop pop pop" of a motor-bike coming up a nearby lane. I took little notice, but soon saw a figure plodding across a field whom I recognised to be the Head Forester. He walked round the fence and joined me to observe the planting activities. Naturally, when the woodmen, and there were seven or eight engaged on this task, saw that the "boss" had appeared, they tended to speed up (they weren't on piece work) and from where we stood they appeared to be pretty active. After a while, the foreman in charge of the gang came across and, peering through the wire netting said, "Are we doing alright sir?".

"Aye it appears to be so," came the Scotsman's reply, "but I'll tell you what, you look like a lot of monkeys in the zoo."

That plantation still goes by the name of The Zoo!

I suppose many woods, countrywide, have been named through similar incidents, but I am familiar with several in a comparatively small area.

One, Jones Wood, got its name because a lady friend of the Head Forester was a Mrs Jones and she was the person who planted the first sapling when the wood was laid out. Simple that one. Another wood, although not really planted to produce timber, has a much more regal name. Around five acres had been planted with Norway spruce, the smaller specimens of which are in great demand at Christmas time, probably more so then than they are today. Many hundreds had been cut and used during the festive season, but as most of those remaining had reached a height unsuitable for Christmas trees, it had been decided to leave them to grow on and become a wood. At that time it was a wood without a name. However, it so happened that quite a large number of pheasants had taken a liking to it, mainly I suppose for the warm roosting, and on one shooting day it was incorporated in the afternoon's sport. A large number of birds went over one gun which did them full justice. At the end of the drive, this particular gentleman asked the name of the wood and, of course, he was told it had no name, having been planted only to provide Christmas trees.

"All woods should have names," he said, whereupon the owner of the estate said, "May I name it after you sir, for you shot the first pheasant driven out of it?"

"By all means, I should be delighted," came the reply.

Ever since, that wood has been called "The Prince of Wales Wood. As I was the keeper who drove the pheasants out it was (almost) my first encounter with a member of the Royal Family!

The names of woods and spinnies are a fascinating subject and no doubt the origin of some of them go back many centuries. Some of the names are quite obvious, like the Cow Pasture, more than likely a wood planted on a piece of land that had always been used for grazing cattle; The Drives, quite common on large estates, often being long, fairly narrow woods which served as a windbreak and shelter along the roadway to the mansion, a blessing I should imagine in the days of horse-drawn transport, particularly when a gale was blowing.

Another wood I know well is called The Klondyke and years ago I enquired about this rather unusual name. An old forester, he would be about a hundred and twenty if still alive, appeared to know the reason. Although now a wood, mainly of poplar, it was originally a withen bed of which there were many when basket-making was a rural art. The withens in those days were cut annually, always during the winter when the sap was down and often when the flood water was down as well, for withens, or willow, like a moist situation and such places are liable to flooding.

According to the old forester, it was only a year or two after the withens had been planted that a gang of men, armed with special knives, were busy cutting and bundling the crop. They each had a task to perform, some cutting, some tying the withens in bundles and some the heavy job of carrying the bundles to firm ground where a horse and lorry could collect them. The men carrying naturally tended to follow the same track and after a while the soft, sponge like soil, was churned into mud. It appears that one of the men was returning from the stacked up bundles, and was picking his way along the churned up path, when he saw something glinting in the wintry sunshine. He bent down, picked it up and after polishing it on his coarse trousers to remove the mud, discovered it was a half sovereign. In his excitement he let out a loud "whoop" which drew the attention of all the workers to him. "Klondyke!" he shouted as his mates came to examine the gold coin in the palm of his hand. There was much excitement, as wages were not much more than half a sovereign at the time, and some of the men started scratching around in the mud with sticks to see if any more coins could be found, but with no luck of course. From then on, that wood became known as The Klondyke.

Another wood always went by the name of the person living in a cottage at the end of it and, in my time, it has had three, if not four, different names. Jack Thomas Wood, Jim Grass's Wood, Minchall's Wood etc..

The Gorse is another name used in a number of locations, often having the prefix of the nearest village, e.g. Waverton Gorse, Saighton Gorse, and so on. Strange as it may seem, neither of those coverts on the Westminster Estate has a single gorse bush. I did once ask an old earth-stopper how such places came to be named. He didn't know, but conjectured that maybe at one time it was just an area of gorse, which may have have been left to harbour foxes. Over the years the gorse may have died out and eventually large patches of blackthorn had taken over and many saplings, oak, ash and birch, thrived, making them into the woods of today. Very feasible, but only conjecture, yet that name "Gorse" still holds good.

There is even a wood on the Estate named from the day I got my nickname, "The Crow". The present Duke's uncle was a very nice man, but always asking hard questions and, on one occasion, I uhmmed and ahhed for a while. "Come on Norman, you're like a damned old Crow," he said. The name stuck and Crow Wood came to be called after me.

Who could hazard a guess at the origin of a wood named The Sourbutts? Perhaps this comes from the 19th century when much heavy land was ploughed in such a way that "butts" were made. Hardly a familiar sight today, but certainly still to be seen in parts of Cheshire. This type of ploughing gave a field the appearance of corrugated cardboard, usually grassland, for the low channels provided good drainage via tile pipes.

I was once talking to an old farmer about such a butted field and he said, "Aye, the old timers weren't daft, even in wet weather the humps were dry, and with it being ridged and butted, it made the fields bigger. Stretch a piece of corrugated card and you'll find that quite true".

Maybe, who knows? The wood called The Sourbutts may have been planted on an area that had been ridged and butted, but still proved to be too wet, in fact sour, so trees were planted to utilise the land.

Then there was The Flesh. How could anyone so name a wood? It is a smallish plantation, right up against what is now a farm, but was previously a foxhound kennels. The hounds, particularly in the past, would have consumed a large amount of flesh of all descriptions, calves, sheep, rabbits, hares, even deer, in fact anything that had died on the farms, or was surplus. There was always plenty of this type of offal available and it had to be kept somewhere. Rather than have this often smelly material in the buildings, a strong frame-work was made and the carcasses would be hung on hooks at quite a height from the ground, safe from foxes. Until quite recently, before the trees were felled in this wood, there were large hooks driven into some of the oak trees (I bet the forester wasn't pleased) and I suppose it was only natural that the kennel lad would be told to "get some flesh", hence the name of The Flesh.

To encounter a worker on the land in the days before the Second World War was often an experience never to be forgotten. Many were such characters, the like of which are indeed scarce in modern times.

Some of these old-timers had a real sense of humour and were frequently egged on by their workmates. Having a "go" at one another was rarely taken in anything other than good part. Simple things often amused.

I recall one bitterly cold winter morning when the woodmen were gathering round their fire. "Where's old Jobie got to this morning? He's a bit late," remarked the foreman. As he finished speaking Jobie could be seen plundering up the track.

"He looks well rugged up," one of the woodmen noted. "Aye," said the foreman, "It be a right cold marnin'."

Jobie joined the circle round the fire. "That there frost be a right stinger this marnin'," he said.

"Aye," they all replied in chorus.

"The missus aint very well this marnin' so I had to light the fire and brew up," said Jobie. "It were so cold in the house, I've got two of everything on."

"What have you got on then?" said the foreman.

"Well I've got two shirts, two pairs of trousers, two westcoats, two jackets and two pairs of socks."

At this point a voice at the back of the gathered men said, "And two pairs of boots eh Jobie!"

This remark raised howls of laughter, but all Jobie said was, "Nay lad, I only got two pair and I didn't want to dirty me going to Church ones."

I recall an encounter with an old, or should it be aged,

woodman (they worked until seventy years of age or more in bygone days). A gang had only just started to "faggot" a wood and the aged woodman was about to start burning the brash. A man had already tied the poles and faggots and stacked them in heaps as he went, so only the waste remained.

When I saw the old lad, he was standing by a silver birch, slowly peeling off strips of the bark. He then moved on to an elder bush and gathered a handful of dead shoots (the ones always full of pith) and also a bunch of dead pieces about as thick as a finger. Staring around him he selected the spot for his fire, between two "stools" that had been cut, but not close enough for the fire to damage them. Using a "pikel" (pitchfork), he cleared the ground and proceeded to light the fire. Just a few slithers of the silver birch bark was the foundation, a match was struck and slowly the silver and red paper-like bark started to burn. As the flames grew, the old lad slowly added the thin, pith-filled twigs from the elder bush. In no time at all the flames were six inches high and the thicker dead pieces were now placed on the fire. Once it had taken hold, a start was made to build the fire proper. Small twiggy pieces of the brash were slowly added and then thicker pieces joined the pile. Soon the flames were leaping a yard in the air, and still more kept being added. When the old forester was satisfied there was enough heat, he stood back and slowly sliced some "Twist" tobacco and rubbed it in his knarled hands.

A pipe was produced from one of his cavernous pockets which was duly filled with the well rubbed "weed". Once filled to his satisfaction, not too tight, not too loose, he bent down and selecting one of the large pieces on the fire, withdrew it and after giving it a rigorous shake, lit his pipe with the glowing end, and as he did so, a glow of sheer pleasure spread across his weathered face. A few puffs on his pipe and he began to pile more fuel on the now fading flames. There was plenty of heat and after a thick puff of smoke and a cascade of sparks, the flames

50

burned through the middle. Watching carefully, I could see the old lad had a method in feeding the fire.

Using his pitchfork he would roll the smaller brash towards him and then place the "sausage" like roll across the fire, each forkful being placed in the same direction, not any old how. Whilst making these rolls, any larger pieces would be deftly put aside and after an area had been cleared, the pitchfork was struck in the ground well away from the fire and a bill hook took its place in his hand. Picking up the larger pieces he held the thinner end over the fire, always ensuring it was lying the same way as the rolls placed there earlier, and normally with one deft stroke of the hook, he would cut through the brash. Should it be a long piece another cut would be required. This system was repeated until all the brash within a reasonable range had been confined to the flames.

I eventually had to enquire as to why what appeared to be such a lot of effort was put into burning what was only really rubbish. "Ah," said the forester. "Tha' saw what I was doing, well I was doing the job proper like. Always lay the brash on across the wind, keep it tidy like. A smaller fire fed right will burn more than a big sprawling one."

"I suppose you're limited on what you can burn on such a fire?" I queried.

"Nay lad. If I had to burn a huge mature tree, a strip or two of birch bark would do me, and only one match, I reckon you noticed that!"

It was fascinating to watch the skill of old country-men, much of which, nay, I suppose most of which, had been handed down from generation to generation.

Some time after witnessing this particular incident, I encountered another gang of woodmen who were working on the other side of the estate, eight or so miles away. There was rubbish to be burned on this site, although a different operation was under way, a patch of woodland was being "clear" felled ready for re-planting. Most of the trees had been taken to the sawmill and these were piles of smaller boughs which were being loaded onto carts, again to go to the sawbench and eventually to end up as logs for the winter. A lot of the rubbish had been burned, but one chap, in his thirties I would think, was just about to start another fire. He already had quite a heap of small brash and was bending over the four feet pile and I could see he was placing the inevitable pieces of birch bark in position. A match was struck and flames began to flicker, and with the addition of further dry twigs, a fire was underway. I looked closely and could see the four-feet "foundation", all more or less lying in one direction across the wind. More dry material was added and slowly the whole pile was in flames. A different method, but the same end result.

I wondered about the different approach and, curiosity overcoming me, I asked the Head Forester who inquired where I had seen the incidents and the names of the men concerned. After some uncertainty he said, "Oh, I know, it's easy. The chappy you saw lighting the first fire was a Cheshire man, born and bred, one of a long line of woodmen. T'other chap was a Shropshire man, been here a number of years now, does quite a few things different than the Cheshire folk, but usually with the same end."

This was most interesting and I suppose it lends weight to that old country saying that there's more ways of killing a cat than hanging it.

Not all encounters with woodmen were in the same vein. Some could be amusing.

It was high summer with lush growth everywhere, bees dancing from flower to flower in search of the precious nectar and butterflies doing the same, but not making such a noise about it. Birds were busy gathering food for their fledglings and then there were the midges, horse flies and the like, all intent on attacking any human who should pass their way. This encounter did not involve any of the foregoing, but rather an insect that was not fond of any human who disturbed it.

Two woodmen were engaged in mowing, with scythes,

the rides through a large and particularly damp wood. Every ten yards there was a ditch at least ten feet wide, and where the ride met the ditch it was crossed on a plank. It was a hot day and mosquitoes, midges, horse flies and "biters" of many colours abounded, so the two men were well covered to protect themselves from bites. Very little flesh could be seen, just a nose and eyes above the handkerchief-covered mouth.

How they worked thus I do not know, for scything is hot work at any time, but they did. As I approached, smoking my pipe and relying on the smoke for protection, there was a man standing, in fact leaning, on the handrail attached to one of the planks. His mate was leaning against a nearby tree.

After conversing with them for a few minutes, I made to go across the plank. At that moment the man at the other end started dancing and shouting. "What's up?" his mate said, as the old lad started to undo his jacket.

He was too busy to reply, for the next moment his trousers were down round his knees and he was running up the track as if he was in a sack race! He wouldn't face the next plank under those conditions and came stumbling back towards us.

"Wasps, wasps," he shouted as he came up to us, and sure enough, there stuck on his "long johns", yes he was wearing long woollen pants, were a large number of that yellow and black demon. The other woodman and myself broke off some bushy twigs and proceeded to brush off the offenders, but the old lad wouldn't stand still and we were dancing round him in an effort to repel the insects.

They were buzzing everywhere, but he eventually plucked up courage and pulled up his trousers and made a dash for the distant plank with, as you may guess, us after him! Further inspection revealed that one or two of the creatures remained to be removed and that duly done, things settled down.

"Have you been stung, Neddy?" I asked.

"Nay, I canna feel any, but that buzzing was enough to drive a mon daft."

"Aye you're right," said his mate, Walter. "You looked real daft with your trousers round your ankles, running up and down the ride."

After a while, and with due caution, a wasps' nest was to be seen where Neddy had been standing and the angry insects must have gone up his trouser legs, despite the fact he had cycle clips on! That must have been a funny scene really, but not very amusing for poor old Neddy, that's for sure. However, despite that, the pair of them were in the same wood the next day and eventually completed the task of mowing the tracks.

The woodmen of bygone days had a variety of jobs to perform during the course of twelve months, from tree felling to mowing, hedgecutting and fencing and they were expert at them all. Once I recall a gang of men, the gang size depending on the job in hand, busy renewing a post and rail fence around a small wood. Not a large wood, more a plantation I suppose it would be called. One side was as straight as a die and the other side curved all the way round. In fact, the wood was a half circle, or letter D shaped, but for some long forgotten reason it went by the name of "Half Moon" wood.

All the timber used for the posts, stakes and rails, had been produced on the estate and matured in the only satisfactory way. Any warped or badly knotted lengths were always cast on one side, for every fencing job had to be perfect. If the fence went in a curve, it had to be a perfect curve, and if it was straight it had to be dead straight, no warped rails to distort the line!

This particular encounter involved once again the Head Forester. As I approached the plantation, I could see the head man coming from the other direction. He was hardly upon the wood when he stopped and shuffled about, almost stooping at the same time. For a few seconds this manouevre puzzled me, then the penny dropped, he was getting himself into position to eye the straight length of the fence. Eventually we met and the "ganger" came up to us. As soon as he was close enough, the boss said, "Jack, you haven't got that fence straight. Come with me."

Off the pair went to the end of the fence and I could see a lot of gesticulating, waving of arms and once a raised voice. Soon they came back towards me, stopped at some distance and the head forester put a stone on one of the fencing posts. After walking at least another twenty yards he stopped and searched around for something to put again on a post, this time with no stone to hand it was a clod of earth. As he got near to me, I could hear him talking to Jack. "I've told you once, you're to pull that length up and make a proper job of it. There's a bend in it now and tomorrow I want to see it straight."

He walked straight past me with just a passing "Good day to you," and it was obvious that his temper was slightly frayed.

"Did you hear what he said?" Jack asked me.

"Aye," I replied. "You've got a bit of pulling down and puting up to do".

"Nay, we wunna be doing that," says Jack. "He'll be gone in a minute, then come with me."

When the Head Forester could be heard disappearing into the distance on his motor bike, we walked to the end of the fence.

"Have a look ye," says Jack.

I did and could not detect the slightest detour from a straight line. "What do you reckon. She's straight alright aint she?" It was a statement with which I had to agree.

"I know what's up wi' boss," he added. "He didn't like those two darkish rails with the light ones in between them I reckon."

The rails in question were in the length the head forester had marked and on a second look they did make it appear a bit out of line. "Aye we'll soon put it right for 'ee."

"What will you do Jack?" I enquired.

"Oh it's easy. Those two rails were bottom of the pile when we started and have soaked up a lot of watter.

"Oh I see," was my answer.

"Aye but boss didn't, nor would he listen."

We walked back to the offending rails and Jack said, "Feel 'em, they be real wet. You wouldn't have noticed in a day or so I bet."

"So what happens now Jack?"

"Oh mon, that be easy" he said as he produced a hammer from his belt and knocked the two wet rails off. "Bring a couple of good rails along here," he shouted to the men now standing round the fire. Two men and two rails appeared and in no time at all they were nailed in position.

Jack turned to me, "Now come and have a look," he said.

Sure enough, when looking along the line of the fence, it did look different, no straighter, but different. "There I told ee didn't I ? That should suit the old lad I reckon, but I must remember to stir the soil up a bit with a spade round those two or three posts in the morning."

"Why?" I asked.

"Well I got to make him think we've had the length up!"

The next time I saw Jack I asked how he went on over the fencing job. "Oh, he be fine and pleased and wondered how we had been so quick."

I wonder if the Head Forester knew what had happened? I've a sneaky feeling that he did, but at any rate I think I must have learned something from that encounter. Would I have remembered it otherwise?

Keeping things straight may seem a strange statement to say about a forester, but there were few of their jobs that were not properly done without that word "straight" coming into it. Planting young trees, normally in straight lines, cutting a hedge with a straight top, if not a straight line, cutting a tree down and leaving a straight or, perhaps more accurately, a level stump or seat, plus those fencing jobs as well.

I once encountered a woodman who was dealing with something else straight, although there was a curve in it as well !

Many woods had quite large numbers of sweet chestnut trees in them and, as with all woodland trees, they eventually reached their life's span and met their fate when the woodman's axe fell. As was the custom when a tree was felled, the "seat" was left, to all intents and purposes, level. In due course, with the passage of time, many of these sweet chestnut trees would send up young growth around the circumference of the seat. When the site of the seat had a good canopy, the young growth was soon drawn straight up to the light. I have explained this so that there will be some understanding of what the woodman was up to. He was making use of some of these young growths, making walking sticks, in fact. It was a common practice to do this whilst working in the woods. Should a seat with suitable growth be found, it would be earmarked until a favourable opportunity prevailed itself. It was no use when the trees were in full leaf and the saplings full of sap. Taken at that time of year, the walking sticks would tend to have a short life, going rotten after only a year or two. Autumn, or "back end" as the men of the woods called it, soon after the leaves had fallen, was ideal.

Whilst working in the area of the earmarked young growth, several suitable lengths would be cut. They had to be the correct size, not too big, not too small and straight, or reasonably so. During the break for lunch, and they had an hour in those days, several lengths of the young sweet chestnut were laid around the fire, not too close but close enough to gently warm up. By the time the sandwiches had been eaten, the sticks had become quite warm.

When I came upon one particular woodman, he was just starting to really warm the thick end of the stick, by holding it well above the flickering embers and by continually rotating it through his hands. I saw, close to the log he was sitting on, a four-inch clay drainpipe and a length or two of fencing wire. Soon the stick was lowered onto the fire, still being gently turned, and then, when the bark started to smoke, it was quickly removed. The drainpipe was standing on end and straight away the thick end of the stick was slowly bent around the pipe. It needed one or two "warmings" before the old lad was satisfied and then the bend, which almost completed a circle, was wired in position. Soon all the sticks round the fire had been treated the same, all wired round that one drainpipe. Each time a stick was wired in position, the woodman removed most of the bark with his knife and it seemed almost to fall off. When all the sticks had been treated thus, they were held over the fire, but not the bent part, only the straight length.

Not a word had been spoken whilst all this was going on, but when he had finished the woodman looked up and said, "Do you want one son?".

I, of course, replied, "Yes please," for by now I had realised it was walking sticks he was making.

"Aye, all reet, they's welcome, but thee have to wait a week or two, I wants to make sure ye has a good 'un."

In due course, I suppose six months later, he called with one of the sticks for me. It had a perfect rounded handle and was as straight as a die. To finish the job off it had been varnished with "knotting".

"Look after 'ee," he said. "It will last you many a long year." And it has!

"You won't find that handle straighten from its curve like them there bought 'uns," he said. "Them bought 'uns is bent by steaming up in a big copper, and that dunna last like one done over a fire. Good day to you young man and thanks for your interest."

What a pleasant encounter that was.

Young sweet chestnut growth seems to be the most suitable type of growth for this treatment, but it is possible to use other saplings. Ash can be bent with great care and really a certain amount of sap in the growth helps. As a rule, ash sticks are left with the bark on, so getting the bark singed does not make for a good stick. Most "ash plants" used by country people are saplings that have been dug up and often the main root is at such an angle to make a satisfactory handle. Failing that, it is often possible to get a good straight stick with a "fork" at a reasonable height and this type is most useful when walking over rough country. Elm, or rather wych or white elm, can also provide material for stick-making and this can be given the same treatment as sweet chestnut, but the resulting stick is not so long lasting. Often an elm "sucker", a shoot thrown up from a large root, will provide a handle from the part below ground. This material usually has the bark removed and is treated with knotting.

Hazel is a handy product and can produce good walking sticks, either simple straight ones, forked ones or the often ornate and artistic ones used as "shepherd's crooks". Hazel is very difficult to "turn", for being a quick grower, the grain is on the coarse side and tends to open up if heated. Much of the bushy type growth in the countryside can produce walking sticks of one sort or another. Blackthorn, a hard, long lasting wood, can only really be trimmed into shape to suit the user, as can holly and yew, but any of these could last a lifetime.

Heads, of one sort or another, were often carved to form the handle. Much time was spent of a winter's night to produce, say a dog's head, out of a thick piece of wood from which a straight piece of growth had been found.

Coming back to that old forester whom I first encountered making sticks, I discovered, several years later, that this was his main hobby and one for which he had a great reputation, people coming from far and wide when in need of a particularly good stick. I called on him one spring evening and he was delighted to show me his collection of walking sticks. They were hanging everywhere in one of the outbuildings, all shapes and sizes and all sorts of timber, some with a high gloss from the varnish and others just as they had been gathered from the woods.

"See them lad," he said, pointing to the untreated ones. "I gotta wait till they be seasoned, daresn't do owt yet, they'd only split when they dried."

He then explained to me the way different types of wood had to be treated and to a degree the proper times to gather them.

"If tha' sees a tidy one any other time, make sure you remember where it is and gather it at the right time. You've still got that chestnut I gave 'ee several years ago?" he enquired. I said, "Yes, of course, it's great".

"Ah well, 'twill always stay that shape, so remember that if you bend any sticks, fire not water every time."

I was writing earlier about a gang of woodmen on a fencing job and the method adopted when the head forester criticised their work, well the following was an encounter on a farm when some posts and rails were being used to stop a gap in a hedge. I heard some voices being raised as I proceeded along a high hedge and thought I recognised one as the farmer. Eventually, I came upon the farmer and one of his men having a bit of an argument about the job in hand. It was mainly about which side of the stakes the rail should be nailed, one said one side, the other said the other side.

The farm labourer said, "If yee puts it the side you say and then puts them there big bullocks in t'field, they will push it off in no time."

"Not if we put them big nails in," replied the farmer, and so they went on. Of course, the farmer had his way and put the rail on the side he wanted. All well and good, but then another stake had to be driven in and once the position had been decided, the labourer started to drive it into the earth with a "mawl" (a large wooden hammer like a sledge hammer).

"Come on mon," says the farmer, "Shape a bit."

"I'm giving it a fair clout," says the farm labourer. "We'm on a big root I reckon, she keeps bouncing back." With that the farmer pulled up the stake, moved it a few inches and said, "When I nod my head, you hit it."

Of course, the labourer knew what he meant and eventually the stake was in firmly, a rail nailed to it and the job finished, but I couldn't help noticing a smile on his face! Several days later, I met the labourer as he was gathering the cows for milking. "What did 'ee reckon of that argument t'other day?" he asked.

"Rather amusing," I replied.

"Aye, it would have been if I'd done what boss said. Mind you, I felt a bit like taking him at his word and hitting him on t'head when he nodded."

*****

Years ago, farmers that grew winter as opposed to "new", early potatoes always used to put them in what was called a hog, well in Cheshire anyway. These were designed to protect the potatoes from frost and were seldom opened should there be frost about.

In areas such as East Anglia, where many acres of this crop were grown, the rows of hogs would stretch for hundreds of yards, but a comparatively smaller acreage in Cheshire did not require such an extensive use of this type of storage. The method of construction involved digging a trench a foot or eighteen inches deep, maybe six feet to eight feet six inches wide, the soil being thrown to either side. When harvesting began, the potatoes would be loaded onto a cart, taken to the hog and tipped into the trench. A farm worker would be waiting for the load, his job being to pile the potatoes up so that there was a ridge running down the hog. Sometimes, if it should be a wet time or the ground was soaked, the crop would be left a day, maybe a couple of days, to dry out. When in a suitable condition, the whole lot would be covered with straw to the depth of maybe six inches. Once covered, the soil was then put over the straw and patted down until quite firm.

Every few yards, a field drainpipe was built into the ridge with a twist of straw inserted in the top. This was to allow moisture out and prevent the potatoes rotting. A fairly dry spot at the side of a field, nearly always the field on which the last crop had been grown was used; if it was too wet, the trench would fill with water and ruin the crop. Rabbits sometimes burrowed into the hog, because it was dry and warm, I suppose, and once an old keeper, George Grass, and myself were deciding what was best to do when the two men, who were responsible for emptying the hog of its spuds, appeared with a horse and cart. We went to have a few words with them, intending to tell them what we were going to do to try and stop the rabbits getting at the potatoes. They looked up and one said: "They be good bakers. I'll sort ee out yer bag full of good uns."

"Oh aye," George said and continued to tell them we were going to deal with the rabbits in due course. We were just about to move off, when the chap shovelling the spuds said: "Ey, here's them big taters for ye."

George Grass looked at him and then said: "Chuck em up on the cart. Them's the Dukes tatties, not yours or mine."

Immediately, a voice behind us said: "Quite right, Grass, quite right."

And who should it be, but none other than Major Kerr who was the Estate Agent at the time.

Old Walter in the hog didn't know what to say or do, but kept shovelling the spuds into the cart, faster, much faster, than he had done before!

We hadn't seen or heard the Major approach, which to say the least was unusual, but he chatted about the rabbit problem and various other aspects of our job.

On departing, he stopped, turned round and said: "Honest men need rewarding. I'll see you get a bag of potatoes, George."

And he did. But I didn't!

Feathered Friends, but not always!

Even when spending most hours of every day out of doors, it is surprising that predators are seldom observed catching their prey. Seed and insect-eating birds are frequently seen, but there are many people who have spent all their lives in the countryside who have not even seen a stoat kill a rabbit, or even a cat take a nestling, so in one respect I have been privileged to have witnessed so much.

Over the years I have watched predators of all sorts at work, from weasels to buzzards, though perhaps a buzzard is not a true predator for it lives on many insects and carrion. However, I have seen one take a young rabbit and also a pheasant poult. Spending a lifetime in the woods and fields means there are bound to have been many meetings with all manner of wildlife, although not half so plentiful these days as before the Second World War. I can only shudder to think what the English countryside would be like without its wildlife.

Many of my encounters, I suppose, would be of great interest to city and urban dwellers, but to me they were almost everyday occurrences. Often there would be a warning that something was afoot, but you had to know the warning calls of many birds, for by and large they are the first to get agitated when a predator is afoot, or on the wing. When a blackbird utters its warning call, it is possible to tell whether it is a predator on the ground or on the wing. A continued "piping" sound is a sure sign that something is moving on the ground, and after long experience it is possible, nine-times-out-of-ten, to be

63

certain what form it will take. Calling "pip pip pip" with great agitation and moving frequently from bough to bough, indicates a largish animal, maybe a fox or a cat. A slightly more subdued calling would probably mean a stoat or even a polecat or mink, but a rather half-hearted calling would more than likely mean a weasel or a rat. When really worried, usually when the blackbird has a nest in the vicinity, some diving down close to the offenders may take place. These are only general descriptions and only long experience enables a person to pick out the finer points.

The blackbird, a good friend to a gamekeeper, has a different call for any winged predator, an often repeated "rit tit titz". This is used for maybe a roosting owl or a member of the hawk tribe perched in a tree or bush. Again this must not be confused with a very similar call used at dusk when the blackbird is about to go to roost. This "rit tit titz" is also used if a blackbird is suddenly disturbed, but then it is repeated very very quickly, obviously because the bird is frightened.

The foregoing should indicate how important it is for a gamekeeper to know all the alarm calls of many birds and it is not only the blackbird that gives out warnings. Every bird has its own language, some I must admit I certainly don't understand. I suppose, in due course, all these various bird calls are hardly noticed, unless there is a reason to do so. Some do bring an instant reaction,

I was still a lad when, one afternoon, I was with a gamekeeper patrolling a large, rather dense wood. We were walking down a broad track when two, or possibly three, blackbirds burst out of the cover and flashed past us, really screaming "rit tit titz", all blended together. The keeper immediately grabbed me and dragged me behind a large "rhody" bush, putting his hand over my mouth as he did so. We stood still, not a sound, and then as another blackbird screamed down the track, the keeper nodded his head. Shortly, a twig snapped and the tension grew. Another twig was trodden on, a smaller one I should think for it seemed closer, but not so loud.

Bembridge Harbour, Isle of Wight, in the late 1920s.

Above: The 2nd Duke of Westminster's yacht, the Cutty Sark, upon which Norman's father, Percy, was the Chief Steward. A fortuitous encounter with the Duke led Norman to serve fifty years as a gamekeeper on the Westminster Estate in Cheshire.

Left: Norman, aged about seventeen, with his younger brother, Douglas.

Norman began his new life in 1929 and Eaton Hall, he remembers, was a massive building, even when viewed from the tradesmen's entrance.

Some of the domestic staff at Eaton Hall in the early years of the 20th century.

There would be eighty to one hundred beaters at the shoots, all of them Estate workers.

The Duke of Westminster's Shoot, in the 1930s.
Above (left to right): Capt. Filmer-Sankey and Brig-Gen.
Sir Joseph Laycock; Mrs Tower and Prince Arthur of
Connaught; the Rt.Hon.Winston Churchill.
Below: Capt. and Mrs E.H.Tattersall;
Maj. Tower and Sir George Thursby.

Keepers based in the Park, in full livery.

The keepers at World's End, near Llangollen. This was a popular shoot with the Duke's guests.

The Dogmen at Aldford.

Top: Norman feeds the birds in "The Torment". Whilst this wood was being planted, the then Gamekeeper, Dick Stark, would regularly check progress. "He's here to torment us again," said one woodman...and ever since it has been known simply as "The Torment".

Above: One of the guests taking a high bird.

Right: Norman selects a cock-bird for the laying pens.

A cherished encounter in Norman's life.
H.R.H. The Prince of Wales presents him
with a long-service medal to mark his fifty
years as a gamekeeper on one estate.

Delivering food to the woods.

Norman and his wife Eileen have lived in the same Estate cottage, in Aldford, since their marriage in 1939.

By the Golden Gates, the Aldford entrance to the Park.

*Old faithful! Norman with his black
labrador, Sam.*

Norman and Eileen, wed for over sixty years.

Nothing could be seen as from our position, behind the "rhody" bush, the view of the track was obscured. Then the sound of rustling leaves made it certain that some person or persons were not far away. The next second the outline of a body could be seen through thin growth and with that the gamekeeper made one dash and confronted the "body". I, of course, followed. There were two of them, both rather nondescript types, one carrying a small bag and the other a spade.

"Gotcha," said the keeper. "I know what your game is. You're after rabbits, ain't you?".

Of course, they had to admit it, even though there were no rabbits to be seen.

"Empty your pockets," the keeper said and both men deposited a number of purse nets on the track. "I'll keep those, and throw the spade down as well, but you say you've no rabbits?"

"That's right," said one of the men.

"You'd better be getting going then," said the keeper, "and think yourselves lucky. If you'd had a rabbit it would have been up those steps at Broxton (the local magistrates court)."

Off the intruding couple of poachers went and in a short while we followed them. Soon they were out of the wood and crossing a field, no doubt heading for their bikes.

"I reckon that pair did have some rabbits," said the keeper. " A few of thee purse nets were damp and did you notice there was fresh soil well up on the spade?. Well let's have a look, we might just be lucky. You search over there and we'll head back down the wood."

Soon the old keeper found a small rabbit burrow that had more or less been dug out.

"Them rabbits they got, by the fur in t'holes, aint far away I bet," he said.

Just in front of me was another large dense "rhody" bush and on peering inside, I could see a couple of rabbits hanging over a bough.

"I knew it," said the keeper. "We could wait for that

pair of devils to come back after dark, but t'aint worth it. Tell you what, you go and fetch that stoat you took out of that trap this morning, we'll leave that for 'em."

I went for the stoat which was hanging up on the hedge at the far corner of the wood and the old keeper produced a length of string and tied it to the bough where the rabbits had been. After a number of days that stoat was still hanging there and we never did know if the poachers had come back to try and retrieve the rabbits.

As far as poachers go, a good deal was learned from that comparatively small encounter. The old keeper had noticed the purse nets were damp, and obviously used, and he'd also seen the wet soil was high up on the spade, suggesting that some recent digging had been taken place. What probably impressed me most was the way the keeper grabbed me and pulled me behind that bush.

I asked him how he knew there was someone in the wood.

"Easy lad," he said. "You heard and saw those black-birds coming down the track? Aye, well them had been disturbed and disturbed blackies do one of two things, dash away as fast as they can and shout, or dash into cover as fast as they can and shout a warning. In a bush or out a bush, I say. If they are coming out of cover, you dive in because there's someone about. If them's going into cover, you dive for your gun - tis a fair bet a predator's after 'em and you might get a shot at it!"

As we proceeded on our way, it crossed my mind that the keeper had taken little notice of the small bag that one of the men had been carrying. The chap had admitted that it held a ferret and I was wondering why the keeper had not confiscated the bag and ferret.

"Well, it's like this," he said. "You've got to know a bit about the law as well as about what the birds in a wood are telling you. If I had taken that ferret, that bloke could have had me in court. The law allows a keeper to take anything like nets but no livestock, so I had to let him keep his ferret."

As an afterthought he added, "I dare say he'll have another spade and some more nets and be out again tomorrow somewhere."

Another incident involving blackbirds also comes to mind, but rather in a different vein.

It was during the severe winter of 1963 when even water pipes, eighteen inches below ground, were frozen up. Many shallow ponds were frozen solid, motor cars were being driven on rivers and much of the wildlife succumbed to the penetrating cold, on top of it being almost impossible to find food. Strangely, it was in the same wood, or rather by the surrounding hedge of that wood, that one of the forestry men was laying a thorn hedge. It had been left to be laid for several years, to grow up to eight or ten feet, but it was getting thin in the bottom with gaps that would allow sheep and cattle to get through.

The chap doing the work had been there for several weeks for there were many yards (or "roods" as he would say) to be laid. When the severe weather started, on Boxing Day 1962, he had been working some time on the job but still had a lot to do. Hardy men those foresters and Walter Huxley, for that was his name, was one of the toughest and there was no way that the weather would deter him from his work. He, of course, always had a fire going and, although only a small one, the heat was intense for it was made out of the dead pieces from the hawthorn hedge and there is not much in the wood line that produces so much heat. This particular day, I went out of my way to call on Walter, to see how he was progressing or, perhaps if I was honest, because that fire I could see flickering from some distance was a great attraction in the severe cold. When I got there, Walter was sitting on a nine-inch clay drainpipe, with a folded sack to make it a bit more comfortable.

We chatted for a while as I warmed my hands and he finished his sandwiches, it being his mid-morning "bagging" time. As he had a few crusts left, I think he saved them deliberately, he broke them into several pieces and threw them on to the bare ground where he had been laying the hedge. The pieces hardly hit the ground before several birds appeared. They did not fly in but hopped, coming out of the bushes where, no doubt they had been sheltering from the penetrating cold. A couple of blackbirds, a thrush (they were more plentiful in those days), even a wren and a couple of great tits, and they all pecked uneasily at the broken crusts, making no attempt to fly off with a piece, as birds usually do.

I said, to Walter, "You've got a bit of company round your fire."

He replied, "Aye, I've been feeding them a bit for a day or two, but there ain't so many as a week ago, some of 'ems died I know."

He then proceeded to fill his pipe, and after getting it going well with an ember from the fire, said, "Aye lad, them's hungry, they'll eat owt. Go up t'hedge about five yards, you'll see."

I got up and after a short distance I came across the remains of a blackbird with its feathers scattered around. The bones had been picked clean, even the smaller ones from the wings and legs.

"What do you reckon has done this Walter, a mouse?"

"Nay not a mouse lad, I'll tell 'ee."

Drawing hard on his pipe and blowing clouds of smoke he said, "Twas yesterday when I sat down for me "bagging" when I saw what was going on. I knew a blackie had died, 'cause it was close to the fire and I threw it up on the hedge, I couldn't burn it. As I was getting me grub I saw two more blackies pecking away at their dead mate, mostly pulling feathers out. I didn't think much of it at the time but I had another look afore I knocked off and found it like you got it in your hand now."

68

"Well I'm blowed," I said. "So you saw them eating it?"

"Aye more or less and them sort of birds ain't cannibals. I reckon won't be many of them left if this cold goes on much longer."

So there we are, when in a fight for survival, I suppose anything goes. It was a most enlightening encounter with Walter that bitterly cold morning. It was an incident, the likes of which I had never come across before and certainly not since.

Birds, at any rate to us, often do what seem unusual things, although probably, as far as they are concerned, are quite rational. I recall one still mellow evening that you sometimes get in September. Some of the leaves on the trees were just on the turn for their autumnal show, pale shades of orange, yellow and brown showing in many places. It was a peaceful scene until suddenly, the stillness of the evening was broken by the alarm calls of numerous birds, starting with that sweet little bird the Jenny wren giving voice in a most excited way. A blackbird soon joined in, then a hedgesparrow and, loudest of all, a jay. I knew at once what was on the move. They were all giving the alarm notes that indicated a winged predator.

I looked around me but could not see anything until I turned my gaze to a long sloping meadow below. There was a hare loping quietly along as if it had just woken from its daytime snooze. I watched it travel a few yards and then the chorus of alarm calls ceased, a sure sign that a winged predator was close. From nowhere, a hen sparrow hawk appeared and, with almost closed wings, struck at the unsuspecting hare. There was a loud squeal from the surprised animal and several large tufts of fur floated in the air. The hawk towered into the sky and then almost closing its wings, again struck at the frightened animal which had been so surprised from the first attack that it had almost remained stationary. Again more fur went flying, but this time the hare moved into "top gear" and dashed away at high speed. After its second attack, the hawk glided up onto a dead bough protruding from an oak tree and remained there for several minutes before slipping off along a hedge, only several feet from the ground and no doubt having a smaller supper in mind.

That was one encounter with a sparrow hawk which I well remember, but I think another is well worth recounting. This time starlings were involved. As is the wont of this particular bird, and many others for that matter during the winter months, they like to have a communal roost, large numbers heading at dusk to a selected wood or even large patches of "rhodies" or osier beds. This particular roost was at one end of a largish wood where dense patches of blackthorn grew. So many starlings were coming to the roost, that many of the adjacent conifers were weighed down with the roosting birds and some of the reasonably supple branches were broken. I was standing just outside the wood, not far from a huge oak growing right in the corner. I didn't go under the tree as I didn't want to be whitewashed!

Hundreds, no literally thousands, of starlings were coming in. Band after band of them and the way they twisted and swirled was a marvel well worth beholding. One second they would be flying straight and then in a split second they would climb or turn in unison, as if a drill sergeant had shouted an order on the parade ground.

The twittering was so loud it drowned out any other sound around and at times the air was black with the birds. If you looked away from the wood, it sometimes seemed as if there was a huge black cloud approaching from some distance away. There was no possibility of hearing anything, other than the chattering of the starlings and the beating of their wings, so when a hen sparrow hawk glided up into the large oak, I didn't hear a single alarm call.

I watched the handsome hawk, wondering what would happen next. I soon found out! As the bands of starlings approached, the hawk left its perch and flew straight into the birds. In a matter of seconds she was back with a starling in her talons. Now what, I thought, keeping my eyes on the predator. It soon became obvious that the starling wasn't intended for a meal because the hawk just jumped a few feet, placed the now dead starling in a large fork of the tree, and without more ado struck out into another large band of approaching birds. The starlings seemed to completely ignore the presence of the hawk in their midst and just kept on coming.

Mrs Sparrowhawk returned to the same perch with her capture and placed it in the fork to join the first. I watched fascinated as, time and time again, the hawk met the starlings, returned to the oak, planted her capture and made another foray. I lost count of the number of birds she had taken, but the fork was full and several dead birds fell to the ground.

This went on for some time, in fact until the light faded and no more birds could be seen approaching the roost, although some could be heard coming in after dark to join their noisy comrades, no doubt having made a long journey to do so. I could not fathom out the reason why that hen sparrow hawk had killed so many starlings, it certainly wasn't to eat, for starlings have a reputation of being unpalatable to almost all predators. The only conclusion I could come to was that the hawk was so busy just for the practice, or was it just for the fun? It's anybody's guess, but I never saw a repeat of that particular encounter with a sparrow hawk.

On another occasion, I was walking along a ride one spring morning and it was a joy to hear the various birds in full song. One side of the ride had a "stand" of conifers, spruce and larch and on the other side was a wide strip of shrubs, mostly privet, but quite a few rhododendrons, also some low growing cover in between. In fact, this particular wood had been planted about thirty years earlier especially for pheasant shooting and the area of shrubbery was the point from which the birds were flushed on a shooting day. With odd patches of briars and here and there clumps of stinging nettles, it was an ideal haven for many small birds and being spring there were numerous warblers around in the ideal nesting conditions. I could hear Garden Warblers, Blackcaps, "Peggy" Whitethroats, a Willow Wren or two, plus some of our resident birds, Chaffinches, Hedge Sparrows, "Jenny" Wrens and on the outskirts of this shrubbery area, a "Grasshopper Warbler", a summer visitor I haven't heard for many a long year.

I stood for a while taking in the chorus of bird song and looking for some of the songsters perched on the topmost twigs of the shrubs, but on the other side of the track in the conifer trees, all was almost silent. There was a wood pigeon "cooing" in the distance and on the outside of the wood, and some distance away, perched I should imagine high up in a tree, a carrion crow giving off its raucous call.

The scene that morning was soon to be changed.

As I started to move off, there came the shrill warning note of a wren from the edge of the conifers. I don't know why, but I looked up and above the line of half-grown trees there appeared a dot in the sky. At that point it appeared no bigger than a full stop on a printed page, but in a split second I could see it was a large sparrow hawk stooping towards its prey... and it was coming as if to hit me!

It didn't, of course, for when it was twenty feet or so away, a chaffinch broke cover and the next thing I saw was a bunch of feathers floating slowly to the ground and a fast disappearing sparrow hawk with the chaffinch in its grasp. I was amazed at the speed of the hawk. It was a cock bird, incidentally, and it appeared as from nowhere and was away out of sight with its capture. I asked myself, why did that chaffinch leave cover? Perhaps, it was my presence that caused it to do so, or was it in an exposed position and was trying to get to thicker cover, with dire results? When I got to the end of the wood, I saw some small feathers drifting down from a fencing post and on investigation discovered that they were cock chaffinch feathers and this was obviously the spot at which the sparrow hawk had "dressed" his meal.

72

I stood a few seconds thinking of a hen chaffinch that had lost its mate. A carrion crow drifted slowly by, and as it passed called .. "arrh", as much as to say, I warned everybody earlier.

That morning, I had encounters with spring bird song, a sparrow hawk and a carrion crow, all linked in one way or another, and I mustn't forget to mention that I nearly put my foot on a Willow Wren's nest which was in a rut on the track. The bird flew off and I could see a number of small speckled eggs in the nest. Days later, I saw the nest again and every egg had hatched.

This encounter though is with a falcon, a peregrine falcon. I had seen them when a lad, killing racing pigeons as they crossed the coastline on a race from France, but this was in Cheshire, at that time some distance from any known breeding area. Only rarely was a peregrine seen and then usually during the early autumn when an immature bird would spend a few days in the area. In those days, there were a number of pairs nesting in North Wales, so it was a wonder more weren't seen in Cheshire, a comparatively short distance as the crow, sorry the peregrine, flies!

February was the month in which, on most sporting estates, pigeon-shooting took place. An effort was always made to reduce the numbers, for with large flocks about there could be a large amount of damage to crops. Winter wheat, sown in the autumn and despite being five or six inches high, could soon be reduced to ground level. This was not very pleasing to a farmer, in a way understandable, but what always rather amused me was the fact that some farmers who kept sheep would turn them onto a field of wheat to graze. It seems though that sown wheat sends up one shoot, but if grazed to the ground can yield up two, three or even four shoots by the time the spring growing season arrives.

Market garden areas probably suffered most from the hordes of pigeons. Any green crop was bound to attract them, sprouts, and spring cabbage always received a lot of attention. Should there be a frosty spell or a fall of snow, it was almost essential to have men scaring the pigeons from the greens, and many market gardeners employed men to shoot them. It was a full-time job for a pigeon is a hungry bird and is feeding all the hours of light during the short winter days.

It was a calm February afternoon for pigeon-shooting and at the appropriate time the guns were making their way to their appointed places, bearing in mind that a successful a pigeon-shoot has to be organised. Every wood must be covered and the guns spaced more or less evenly through the wood. Strict instructions were given that very high birds were not to be shot at. Patience was important, wait until the birds were low enough to be sure of a kill, i.e provided the guns could actually hit them !

As I watched four guns, all local farmers, making their way to their appointed spots in the large wood, I wondered what the bag for the evening would be, for at that time there wasn't a pigeon in sight. The wood was a well known roost for pigeons, but a bad wood to gather the birds killed, for there were many wide drainage ditches. The guns were getting deeper into the wood and as they progressed, now and again could be heard the "quack" of a mallard as it rose from one of the ditches. I had not gone more than twenty yards when I heard the familiar "whistle" of a band of teal as they too were disturbed from a ditch. They passed right overhead and I watched them as they twisted and turned as if one bird. Passing overhead several times, they eventually disap-peared as they went down, obviously to settle on a nearby pond.

Soon the pigeons began to arrive but, being a calm evening, passed over several times out of range of the guns. Eventually, patience paid off and once they decid-ed to settle, the wood rang with a barrage of shots. All went quiet for a while, but 'ere long the grey flocks returned to be met once again by gun fire. This was repeated several times and dusk was fast closing in on the scene, when once again I heard the sound of airborne teal. They approached me flying quite high and it went through my mind that they were away to their feeding grounds. That may have been the case, but their journey was interrupted. There was sudden panic and the "band" split into a number of small groups and as they did so I could see the reason - a falcon, a peregrine falcon, was fast approaching. The teal twisted and turned, but the falcon, with unerring accuracy, struck.

A bunch of feathers floated slowly down as falcon and teal, appearing to be locked together, almost hit the top of some oak trees. The peregrine recovered in time and quickly climbed into the sky and disappeared into the descending dusk. I could hear the rest of the teal calling, but did not see them again.

People see a lot of big black birds feeding, maybe on a stubble, and will say "look at those crows", but they are not technically correct. I don't doubt for a moment that there are some carrion crows amongst the band, but you can be certain that the vast majority are either rooks or jackdaws. The carrion crow tends to be a much more solitary bird. Unlike the rooks which nest in large numbers in a "rookery", the crow usually picks a tree which is out in the open. They will join other "crows" (rooks and jackdaws) in a communal roost, but even then they are late arrivers, coming in when it is practically dark.

I remember some time ago, whilst touring round the Cotswolds, we came upon a large stubble field which was in the process of being ploughed. There were a large number of "black birds" feeding and a good many seagulls following the plough, as they are wont to do. We got out of the car and over a dry stone wall watched their antics.

A lady in the party remarked, "I wonder what a cross between the black ones and the white ones would be like?" An instant retort from an older lady, a bit of wit, was, "The Black and White Minstrels!" I suppose you can call this an encounter, but I hope it's not taken as "racist".

Coming back to the crows, carrion crows I mean, they are certainly very efficient predators. At certain times of the year they feed mainly on carrion, but they are not a bird to miss any opportunity. Spring will see crows hunting hedgerows in search of birds' nests and, if not in too dense a situation, it's goodbye to those eggs. Ground nesting birds, pheasants and partridge, even when the hen bird covers the eggs, are also vulnerable. Green plovers also received a lot of attention from carrion crows during the nesting season and despite their frantic attempts to drive them away, it is nearly always the black villain that wins. The nests of moorhens, coots, and even skylarks are robbed and later on the fledglings are taken.

The following encounter, early one morning, involved a carrion crow and a moorhen chick. It was a lovely late May day and all the countryside was so fresh looking as I walked along the riverbank where the hawthorn bushes were in full blossom, pink, white and dark red... a lovely sight.

Now and again, rearing its head above the lush riverside growth, could be seen the tall spike of a foxglove, hardly in flower but the largest buds were just showing some colour. Many other water loving plants were in bloom and filled the still air with perfume. A moorhen or coot would scuttle across the river, looking as if it was almost walking on the water, and often following behind would be the "tribe", six or seven little black balls of fluff, following their mother with the greatest of haste.

After following the river for almost a mile, and stopping frequently to admire the vista, I came to an "Iron Bridge", a highly arched bridge which carried the drive from the "big house". Wishing to be on the other bank of the wide river I proceeded to the apex of this marvellous structure which still stands and is at least 150 years old.

The view from this point was well worth admiring. Downstream, on either bank there were mature trees, one or two beech, several oak and a number of poplar, all with their fresh leaves showing up well in the early morning sun, and in places the riverside willows with their branches touching the water. Leaning for some time on the balustrade of the bridge, I was watching the current below taking various small items with it on its way to the sea. Mostly small twigs were floating beneath me, but I did see one glass beer bottle and a small plastic container of some sort (not much plastic about at that time). Lower downstream I saw a coot swim sedately from one side to the other, not a chick in sight, and then a mallard, paddling along quietly close to the bank, with a string of ducklings in tow.

As I watched or rather caught the occasional glimpse of this happy family, a moorhen set off across the river at full speed, followed by several chicks. I'm not sure how many, for things happened so fast. The moorhen reached the far bank calling all the while and the chicks started out on what, to them, must have been a long journey. The leading chick was about eight yards out into the river when, from nowhere, a carrion crow swooped. It hit the water with a splash, but the next second was making for a large beech with a fledgling moorhen in its claws. The other youngsters bobbed under the water and quickly joined their parent who was frantically calling them. I don't know where the crow came from except above and I can only conjecture that it had glided silently and unseen into one of the riverside trees, just to wait its chance. As I pondered this encounter, I wondered how many more youngsters the black villain would have. It had certainly perfected this method of getting a feed.

A great friend of mine, Joe Pemberton, had a rather unusual experience some time ago, in which the problem was also a carrion crow. Joe is a retired police officer and for many years had been a churchwarden at the village church. His duties entailed daily visits to the church, which unlike many churches these days, was left unlocked during the hours of daylight.

Unfortunately, Joe had lost his eldest son not long before the crow incident, so when he was around the church, he would often pay a visit to his son's grave. This particular day, he was some distance from the grave when he heard the rattle of metal on stone. His first thought was that there were vandals about or youngsters up to no good.

He proceeded with caution in an effort to find out the reason for the noise, but when he got in sight of his son's grave, there was no sign of anyone about; in fact, it was so quiet that he caught a glimpse of a crow flying through the boughs of the large yew trees.

He could also see that flower containers on some of the graves had been thrown around and, as several were made of aluminium, this was the cause of the metallic sounds.

The next day, Joe returned to inspect the scene of the previous day's disturbance, only to find a repetition of the chaos. The time had come for action, for not only had the floral tributes been thrown around, but there was mud splashed over a couple of the black and shiny headstones and "whitewash" on the top edge of another. This new twist in the scene, of course, put the idea in Joe's mind that the crow might well be the culprit.

That same evening, we were having a quiet drink in the "Greyhound", when Joe recounted these incidents to me and he wondered whether I thought the crow could indeed have been responsible.

"I don't doubt it for a minute." I replied. "Jackdaws and magpies are well known for taking shiny objects to their nests and crows are of the same family."

"I'll have to make an early morning visit," Joe said, adding: "with the gun!"

On our next meeting, I asked Joe if he had had any success.

"None at all," was the reply. "I've seen the crow on most visits, but have been unable to get a shot."

"Don't shoot until you are sure," I said. "Should you miss, your chances of getting the devil will have gone."

"Something will have to be done," he said. "I keep putting the flowers and plants back and even wash the headstones, but it's just as bad the next visit."

About a week later, we met again and Joe said: "I hope you've got an idea as it's still going on."

I had thought of a plan that might work and outlined it to Joe, but I won't go into the details (trade secrets!). He was a bit sceptical to start with, but said he would give it a go.

A couple of days later, he phoned to say the problem of the 'black marauder' had been solved. The crow was dead.

"The parson wanted to know how I had managed it, but only us two will know that," he chuckled.

So here endeth the tale of the churchyard crow.

However, only a week or two after Joe had reported his success, I was attending a funeral at a church, not more than three miles away as (well, it is a saying), the crow flies! It was a real old country church, with ancient yew trees spreading over ancient graves. The ceremony was over and as I wended my way around the graves, I came across one with fresh flowers scattered around. I immediately thought of Joe's problem. There was a difference though; there were no metal flower vases pulled around, just a two-pound jam-jar which had been sunk into the ground... a bit beyond a crow's ability, that! Anyway, I would hardly think there were two crows at it. It seemed most unlikely, so I wandered on.

The first yew tree I came to had "whitewash" (a crow's droppings) down the trunk and moving gently in the breeze not yards away was a feather, a black one. Without a doubt, it was a crow's. I'll let readers draw their own conclusions.

Animals, large and small

Documentaries are often made about most of the larger animals, foxes, badgers and the like, but there are many smaller inhabitants of the countryside that have received little attention. Take the weasel, for instance, a charming little member of quite a large family that includes stoats, polecats, pine martins and others. The following encounter with the smallest member of that tribe was rather amusing, but completely unsuccesful as far as the weasel was concerned.

I was leaning against some rails which filled a gap in a hedge, actually watching several hares doing their usual dancing and sparring as they are wont to do during the month of March, "as mad as a March hare" as the saying goes. I must have been stationary, hardly moving for ten minutes or more, when I heard a wren start up with its alarm call, a trilling oft repeated. The bird was some distance from me but I was almost certain, by the rather subdued sound of its call, that it was a weasel at work, not a stoat. Sure enough, I spotted the mouse-like animal rearing itself up a yard or so from the hedge, its cream-coloured chest shining in the weak spring sunshine. Soon it disappeared into the bare hedge and I turned my attention back to the frolicking hares.

As I glanced their way, the playtime had broken up and two of them were heading my way as if they intended to go through the gap in the hedge where I stood. Remaining motionless, I was not surprised to see them coming closer and closer but, when within about ten yards, the leading hare spotted me and changed course, making for the hedge between me and where I had last seen the weasel, obviously aware that there was a gap to run through. The next thing, there was a loud squeal from the hedge bottom and then the hare appeared, dancing and jumping about, at times leaping high in the air. I watched intently at this performance and caught glimpses of the weasel on the hare's back, just behind the long ears, hanging on for dear life.

Naturally, it was an uneven battle and when the pair got ten yards or so out in the field, the little mammal fell off and scurried as fast as it could back to the hedge. The hare legged it as only a hare can, following a zig-zag course as if pursued by a dog. Hard luck, little weasel, you certainly took on something a bit too big for you to manage that time! I wondered afterwards if weasels ever do kill hares. Leverets maybe, but who really knows? There is always a doubt with me after that incident.

Sadly, there are few otters in the English rivers and streams although otter hunting ceased many years ago. At one time, most streams of any size were at least visited by otters, even if breeding didn't take place there.

One lovely spring morning in the mid-1930s, I was strolling along one of the many woodland tracks, listening to the song of the warblers. Not far away, I could hear the calls of hunger from young herons as the parent birds returned with a gullet full of fish.

Now and again a moorhen would slip quietly off its nest as I approached, for on each side of the tracks were wide ditches, or channels. Only a slight ripple disturbed the water when the bird left the nest full of eggs but, by looking carefully, sometimes a head, with the distinctive red top to its bill, would surface, only to disappear again in an instanct.

There were no fish in the wide channels, although originally these were quite deep. Over the years they had gradually filled up with leaves from the numerous oak trees, often leaving little more than a foot of water. At each point where a track crossed a channel, there was a wide plank and a handrail, the latter certainly needed for in many cases the crossing was anything up to fifteen feet wide.

I came to one of these planks and though the "biting" insects were not so numerous as later in the year, I paused for a rest and lit my pipe, the smoke from which was a deterrent to the few insects about. I had hardly been leaning against the handrail for five minutes when I heard a distinct and rather piercing whistle from further up the wood. For a moment I thought it was another keeper or a woodman trying to locate me and then realised it did not quite sound like a human whistle, at least not like any I had previously heard. Again the whistle pierced the still air and this time it seemed much closer. I knew then that it was an otter afoot and it was quite plainly coming in my direction. Keeping perfectly still, I hoped I would catch a glimpse of the normally elusive animal, or maybe more than one, for I was now certain it was a mating call I was hearing.

After a short while I heard, what I can only describe as a "grunting squeak", coming from around the bend which lay ahead. Almost immediately an otter appeared, with another in close pursuit. I never moved a muscle, for the pair were heading straight for the plank on which I was standing.

One came onto the plank with what I suppose you would call an "up and down gait" and went straight over my feet. The second one slowed up as it reached the plank, came to a stop and sniffed the air, uncertain I suppose whether it was safe to cross or not. I expected this one to slip into the murky water below me and disappear, but no, after a few seconds it plucked up courage and came onto the plank and also crossed my feet.

I watched it make its way up the track and out of sight, followed once again by that piercing whistle. It's years since I last saw an otter, not unusual you may say, but I hadn't even seen a "track" (footprint) until quite recently when I spotted where one had obviously crossed a muddy patch on a brookside. Let's hope this fascinating creature is making a comeback.

Stoats are another creature of the countryside, very similar to the weasel, but I would think it is at least twice the size. If in doubt, a certain way to tell one from t'other is the long tail of the stoat. This always has a fluffy jet-black tip, whereas the weasel's tail is only short and a uniform colour with the body. Stoats will change their colour, particularly on high ground where snow may lie for most of the winter. They turn white, or creamy white, "Ermine", and their skins are much used for ceremonial dress, but the tip of the tail always remains black.

A very lively and inquisitive animal is the stoat, but often very destructive too. Their main food is rabbit, mice and the like, but during the spring, many birds and eggs are taken. It's obviously not a very popular animal with gamekeepers, as an awful lot of gamebirds can be taken by a litter or two of stoats, the young getting particularly hungry when there are still plenty of young pheasants about.

Stoats keep together as a litter until they are full grown and fully capable of looking after themselves. As a rule they are born underground in a disused rabbit hole, often in the hollow stump of a tree and at times in a dry stone wall. A favourite place many years ago was a hayrick, one that was being kept from one season to another. Nice and cosy in there, no doubt, and maybe plenty of mice about for when the youngsters started to take solid food. I once encountered a litter of eleven in such a place. There they were, well a couple of them, just about half-grown, popping their heads out of holes at ground level. First one and then the other would appear, but neither came completely out. After a while, a black-bird's alarm note could be heard in a nearby hedge and sure enough another appeared, but this was an adult stoat, carrying, what seemed to be a mouse. There was a sharp squeak from one of the youngsters who was in hot pursit as the parent vanished down the hole. I thought that was the last I would see of them, but then one head popped out again and then another, and then another. In no time at all, heads were appearing and disappearing in the many small holes at the base of the rick. I thought there were five or six youngsters, a normal litter for a stoat when food is plentiful, but in fact as they dashed out into the open to play, there were eleven and they seemed to be everywhere, dashing hither and thither and fighting in ball-like heaps.

At one point, they all stopped their activities at the same moment, as if a whistle had blown, but quickly resumed their play, which wasn't play really, of course. They were in the process of building up muscle and reactions for the time when their lives would depend on them catching their own food. Suddenly, everything was brought to an abrupt conclusion by a loud squeal from halfway up the side of the rick. As if each youngster was on elastic, they disappeared into the holes and when I looked into the rick I could see an adult stoat leisurely moving away, as if it had been watching all the time.

It was often possible to hear the squeal of a rabbit almost anywhere in the countryside when these animals were numerous, so numerous in fact that at certain times of the year, and just before dusk, the fields were covered in browsing conies. A clap of the hands and it would seem as if the field was on the move. I suppose nature, being what it is, ensured that predators had a good reproduction rate, for when there were plenty of rabbits, there were certainly plenty of stoats and the like.

One early mid-July morning, a real summer's morning at that, my duties caused me to be walking the river bank, the Welsh Dee, although I was actually in Cheshire. The sun was glistening on the water as it flowed slowly towards the sea and, now and again, a fish would break the mirror-like surface as it took a small fly. In the distance I could see a family of moorhens paddling sedately across a wide point in the river and all seemed peaceful and quiet as the inhabitants of the countryside started on their daily routine. About twenty yards away, upstream, a waterhen called its alarm note and then, suddenly, appeared on the water. It called again and then made a dash for my side of the river, with flapping wings and flaying legs it appeared to walk on the water. Being July, the riverside growth was pretty dense and apart from a few places where cattle had been down to drink, it was impossible to see any movement. In a matter of minutes or so, another moorhen did the same as the first, only several yards nearer to me, and my eyes were drawn to a fairly large watering place surrounded by briars. I could just discern movement and then a glint of white as a stoat rolled over and plopped into the water. In seconds the whole family were following and swimming straight towards me. They looked just like a string of sausages as the line swung slightly from side to side with the gentle current. Keeping "line astern" they came closer and closer as the movement of the river brought them to land below where I stood. I counted them as best I could and there were certainly six, or possibly seven. Mother stoat was taking her litter to pastures new!

On another occasion, I was actually watching a hen sparrow hawk towering high in the blue sky, making use of every thermal on a lovely day. Out of the corner of my eye, I caught sight of a rabbit making a rapid retreat from one place to another. My gaze was naturally diverted by this movement and when I looked skywards again, the sparrow hawk was just a faint dot high in the blue sky. The quick movement of that lone coney now drew my attention, for although it had disappeared, I could hear the " kweet" of a willow wren indicating the presence of a ground predator. There was plenty of ground cover, mainly tufts of course grass and patches of nettles, but closer to me was a massive oak tree which must have been several hundred years old. At the base were several rabbit holes between the spur roots, and there were also small holes about eight feet from the ground, where boughs had rotted off over the years.

There was no sign of any movement as I stood watching and listening but, just now and again, the warning note of the willow wren seemed to be coming slowly closer. It is not easy to judge whether a bird giving warning of a ground predator is in front of or behind the animal, but, as a rule, the birds are behind if the predator is moving rapidly and in front if it's slowly hunting. I was certain the cause of the alarm was eight or ten yards away, but I was wrong for suddenly two well-grown young rabbits bolted from the roots of the oak. From inside the hollow tree I could hear rustling and scraping followed by the appearance of a stoat, its head looking this way and that.

To my surprise, it leaped a foot in the air as a rabbit behind tried to emerge from the same hole. The stoat bolted in great haste and went out of sight round the tree with the rabbit in pursuit. Round and round the tree went the stoat and the rabbit, though how many times I don't know, for even I was getting dizzy watching these antics. Eventually, one had to give up and it was the stoat and as I watched and waited she (I was certain it was a bitch) half appeared through one of the small holes up the tree, her low chattering giving the game away. With one gigantic leap, she left the tree and landed amongst some tufts of grass before just melting into the cover.

I looked to the base of the tree and there sitting calmly in the mouth of a hole was the rabbit, a scruffy specimen, and as it scratched itself I could see it was a doe and there was much loose fur on her chest. That was the answer. The old doe wasn't going to let a stoat have her young, so she took the only action available... she gave chase. So, that was one time when a rabbit defeated a stoat, but I bet it doesn't happen very often, and anyway, the stoat couldn't have been that hungry.

Much has been written about foxes and badgers, but I suppose a "tome" of this nature would not be complete without a paragraph or two about what, to most people, are considered much-loved animals. It was during the year or two when "mixxy" (myxomatosis) devastated the rabbits of this country. No matter where you went, you would see the remains of conies. Some, still alive, would be hopping about aimlessly, unable to see where they were going, their eyes closed with the swelling of the head.

There were rich pickings for scavengers like carrion crows which were in their element, food strewn everywhere for them. Magpies were the same and it was no trouble at all for them to get breakfast, lunch and evening meal. Other smaller birds and animals also took advantage once the remains of the rabbits had begun to decompose and there were beetles and insects to be found in the heaving carcasses. Badgers took great advantage of this situation, for there is nothing they like better than a feed of large, fat, juicy beetles and with "mixxy" they certainly didn't go short .

When we came upon a rabbit that was obviously on its last legs, we would put it out of its misery and, if any cover was available, place it out of sight. It was a task that soon became depressing and I have to admit that I did not always go very far out of my way if I saw a rabbit.

This encounter involves a fox that at first, I thought, was helping me dispatch the suffering bunnies. Leaning on a five-barred gate, apart from the remains of a rabbit or two in the middle distance, the scene was most attractive. The land fell away from me until it came to a small brook which could be plainly heard as it babbled over some stones. Beyond the brook were fields of different hue, some green, some not so green and others that had been under the plough. It was what one would call a typical countryside scene, or at least it seemed so.

I started to move away and as I did so, I seemed to trigger off a raucous chorus from the carrion crows. They were some distance away, mostly centred around a hedgerow oak, and fine and agitated they were. It must be something large, I thought, to get such a large gathering of crows, maybe a stray dog, too much noise for a cat, but much more likely a fox having a daylight stroll. I returned to my position by the gate post, interested to know what all the racket, coming my way, was about.

Ere long, I saw a beautiful fox coming down a hedge which intersected the brook below me. It appeared and disappeared into the hedge and came out onto the grass field, clearly carrying something. It was a rabbit and I wondered if the fox would stop and start to eat and then it occurred to me that it was carrying a "mixxy". The fox kept coming almost straight at me and, when head on, looked almost like a yellow labrador or golden retriever making a perfect retrieve with the rabbit in its mouth. About thirty yards away, the fox turned to the left and slowly headed for what was another rabbit.

When it reached the unfortunate animal, it simply stood over it with the original capture still in its mouth and, after a few seconds, it placed the first rabbit alongside the second one, stood for a moment, gave a good shake and then came back towards me. This time it was much closer, not more than twenty yards away and from the size and appearance it was a dog fox. Right opposite to me he paused, shook its head up and down and then sideways before moving off at a steady gait.

I went to see the rabbits he had been at and they were both were still alive. There they were, lying side by side with only a short time to live. It was impossible to tell which one the fox had "handled" for the fur on neither of them was even wet, as I had expected. I duly dispatched the suffering pair and as I deposited them in a nearby burrow, I wondered if that fox came back past me deliberately and was trying to tell me something when it was shaking its head.

The instinct for survival is always strong and none more so than in the fox, as illustrated so many times when hunted by hounds. The most natural thing for a fox to do, I suppose, is to find a hole to "go to ground". This, of course, is why the Hunt has "earth-stoppers", men whose duty it is to go round the night before the hounds meet and stop all holes, including large drains, known to be favoured by foxes. With most of the escape routes closed, a hard-pressed fox is liable to hide anywhere, under or even in a hen house or shed, on a low roof, up a tree, and it is not unknown for one to hide in a house if it is lucky enough to find the kitchen door open.

One December, when the local hounds were meeting at the White Horse, a local pub of course being the ideal alternative venue for a "stirrup cup" when the Hunt has not been invited to the big house. After everyone had imbibed in the usual toddy, the Master took the hounds to a nearby wood for the first draw, it having a reputation for always holding a fox. Sure enough, the hounds had no sooner entered than out went Reynard, with much "alloaing" from the attendant followers. Over the fields and fences went the pack, with the field in hot pursuit and ere long could be heard in the far distance.

"They'll make a good point with yon fox," said an old local who was standing in the lane watching (not having been offered a lift by any passing car following).

"Aye, t'will be four or five mile easy, they always has a good run from yon cover," he added.

Time went by and all went quiet, so the two or three spectators dispersed, more than likely to the White Horse. An hour or so later, the hounds and hunt reappeared, not in full cry though and I could see the pack casting in search of some scent, and they were coming in our direction. I was in the stockyard of the Grange Farm, talking to the farmer. "Hey up, looks like a fox is around somewhere," he said.

The hounds arrived in the farmyard and were sniffing everywhere, around the stables, pig stys, the bay full of hay in the stockyard, even the garage, but not once did a hound give tongue. The huntsmen arrived. "Have you seen him?" he asked, but all he got was a negative reply.

"We've lost him then I reckon," he added.

"You been on the same one all the time then?" asked the farmer.

"Aye we reckon so. He gave us a good run, so I lift my hat to him," which he duly did.

With that, the hounds were called together and moved off, probably to make another draw although it was afternoon and time was getting short. After chatting with the farmer a while longer and refusing the offer of a cup of tea, "I'm having one," he said, "twill soon be milking time", I set off about my business.

About half past three, I returned to the farm to collect my bike which I had left in the stable. As I entered the yard, I could hear the milking machine and the occasional blart from a cow demanding to be fed. Just at that moment, the farmer's wife came out, off in her car to collect the children from the village school.

I heard the engine turn over, but it didn't fire, and then with the second attempt it roared into life with an unearthly screaming noise. I had never heard anything like it before, but in a matter of seconds I knew the cause of the problem. Out of the garage dashed an animal that at first glance could have been a brown dog but, as it shot round the corner and down the drive, I could see it was a fox and it had only half a brush!

The farmer's wife appeared rather shaken at the garage door.

"What was that?" she asked.

"It was a fox," I replied. "It must have been holed up in the garage."

"It seemed to come from under the bonnet," she said.

By this time, the farmer had come from the shippon to investigate. "Let's have a look," he said, entering the garage. All seemed in order, but his wife repeated, "It seemed to come from the front of the car."

The farmer lifted up the bonnet and it was obvious where the fox had been hiding, for pieces of fur could be seen in several places and, on the fan belt, there were three or possibly four inches of its brush.

"Well I'll be dammed," said the farmer. "I wonder if it was the one them hounds were casting around for a bit ago?".

"The garage door was only open a few inches," said his wife.

"Looks like it was just enough for him to get through anyway," said the farmer as he took another look under the bonnet. "Ah well, he's cleaned some muck off the engine. Start her up and see if she goes."

The engine roared into life. "Sounds better if owt," said the farmer as his wife backed out the car and set off to collect the children.

This was a rather unusual encounter with Reynard, but what amused me was a report the next spring, of a vixen with cubs, in a wood a couple of miles away... a vixen with a "docked" tail at that.

Fox hunting is one way that helps to control the number of foxes and, of course, the Master of Foxhounds likes to emphasise this. The hounds were meeting in a village, right in the centre of the farming community where they were always welcome. At the Meet were most of the farmers and their wives and a good many of the farm labourers who had been reminded by their bosses, "Dinna forget milkin' time be at three o'clock."

Even the schoolmaster had the children lined up at a discreet distance to take in the splendour of the scene although, no doubt, they had to write an essay about it before the week was out. The horsemen were gathering, some in scarlet, some in hacking jackets, some on top-notch hunters and some on horses that looked rather as if they had just come out of the field, but all were welcome. The Master appeared just before the appointed time to move off and was handed his stirrup cup and from his vantage point, he surveyed the scene, nodding to one, passing the time of day with another. Then he saw, at the edge of the crowd, the man he wanted, and he edged his horse across to him.

91

"Good morning Togo," was his greeting. "Mornin' Master," came the reply.

"Now Togo, you will know. Where will we find the fox that's killing the poultry hereabouts, and the odd lamb they say?"

Togo was the earthstopper and knew the situation regarding fox earths for miles around, where every fox was likely to be and what those foxes had been up to.

"Ah, I know the one you mean Master, a vixen it be and I reckons you should find her in Platts Rough."

"Good man," the Master replied, "We'll draw there first, I would like to deal with that problem."

In due course, the field moved off and soon the hounds were entering Platts Rough. In no time at all they were away in full cry, but it was short lived for everything came to a halt as the fox went to ground. Togo was soon there as the hounds milled around the offending hole, a large rabbit burrow at the bottom of a dry ditch.

The Master looked at Togo who said rather sheepishly, "I looked along here yesterday Master, that hole must have been full of leaves."

"Leaves maybe yesterday Togo, but fox now," said the Master. "We'll leave you to deal with it and move on".

"Very good, Master," Togo replied and with that the field moved on and left him surveying the scene. He removed his jacket and stuffed it down the hole and after looking to see if there were other escape holes, he headed for the nearest farm, a field away, to get a spade. Soon he was back and starting to dig, a task he soon found was not going to be easy for it was all heavy clay and the hole at the bottom of the ditch was a good five feet below field level. As time went on, one or two joined him in the task, but most spectators had gone on following the pack. The terrier man arrived with his charges hoping to be of some help, but Togo would have none of it.

"This is a single hole, it don't go far, we dunner want no terrier in there," he said.

The digging continued and after an hour or more little progress had been made. Several men were taking turns with the spade, but Togo was in the excavation when a gentleman on horseback arrived. He was either calling it a day or on his way to change horses.

Looking down from his lofty perch he said, "Any luck Togo?"

"No sir. It be heavy going here, clay, proper clay, you can hardly cut it with the spade."

"Are you anywhere near it?" the gentleman asked.

"Not yet," said Togo as he threw a spade full of clay up the bank.

"I'm sorry, but I've been thinking," said the gentleman. "You ought to have a J.C.B. for that."

Togo looked up from his labours, face smeared with mud, "No thank 'ee sir. I don't want no decorations - I do this for love."

This remark left the gentleman speechless, but as he moved away a huge smile crossed his face and as he passed me I could see he had a job to stop bursting with laughter. I left soon after and I never did know if the digging party got to the fox. In any event, there did not seem to be any more reports of poultry being killed and, knowing Togo, I would say he achieved success in the end.

Mainly Gentleman, of night, and day !

Poaching has been a rural pastime I suppose for centuries and over that long period things have changed a great deal. At one time, it was mostly deer that were the object of any foray into the forests. With the deer belonging to the King, penalties were heavy, but many cottagers still got their feed of venison. As the years passed and game birds became more plentiful, and were also reared, they became the target of night prowlers. Rabbits were always a popular feed of the rural community and often received the attention of poachers, so I will attempt to recall some of my encounters with such folk over the past fifty or so years.

The first "run in" I can remember was with a single poacher, although they usually operated in twos or threes. I was not very old at the time, in my early teens. It was a lovely September afternoon, the sun was showing the russet and red tints on the leaves and some of the ground cover was beginning to lose its density, the early frost making the rabbit runs plainly visible.

My object was to see if anyone (often locals looking for a meal, for times were hard) had set snares on these runs. There wasn't a sign of a snare and it didn't appear as if any had been recently used either, for when a rabbit is snared it generally leaves a distinct mark where the grass or herbage has been flattened. As I moved along the outside of the wood, I heard a rabbit squeal. Ah, a stoat, I thought, and then it squealed again and I knew at once by the sound that it was no stoat. I looked intently into the wood, but couldn't see any sign of

94

anything untoward, but proceeding slowly, I came to some rails across a gap in the hedge. I climbed over onto quite a wide track inside the wood. Proceeding with caution and being careful not to tread on a twig, which if it cracked would betray my presence, I suddenly saw a man bending down.

I could see he was obviously putting a purse net over a rabbit hole. I moved slowly towards him, but when I was about twenty yards away, he must have sensed my presence, for he turned round. I shouted, "What are you doing?". I got no reply but he at once came rushing towards me. I could see he was not holding anything in his hands, so the danger wasn't too great... and I did have a stout walking stick.

He rapidly came closer and I thought, "He's going to head butt me", and then he was upon me. As he came within a yard or so, I jumped to one side and as his speed carried him on, I pushed with my stick with all my might between his legs. You can guess what happened, he went flat on his face! I jumped across quickly and put my foot firmly on the middle of his back, standing there like you sometimes see them in the wrestling ring these days.

"It's a fair cop, guv" the chap said. "Let me up I won't run".

I suppose I had no option, so I took my foot from his back and he got to his feet.

"What's your name?" I asked him and he gave it to me immediately. He was a well known local boxer who, soon after this incident, went on to win a title fight.

He extended his hand, saying, "Shake. You pulled a good trick on me because I intended giving you a going over," ... which no doubt he could have done. I asked him how many rabbits he had caught and he replied, "Only two, I haven't been here long."

Of course, I could have taken the rabbits and nets off him, but he would have retained his ferret which was still in the small rabbit burrow.

"Come on," I said. "Gather up your bits and pieces" and we went back to where the ferret was still underground. He started picking up his nets and putting them in a heap on the ground and as he went to the last one, a rabbit bolted into it, quickly followed by the ferret. He grabbed the rabbit and quickly dispatched it, placing it alongside the two he had caught earlier .

"Right," I said. "On your way and don't let me catch you here again."

He started to move off saying, "Thanks, thanks very much."

I called him back and said, "Take your tackle and the rabbits with you."

He was surprised, came and shook my hand again and said, "You're a toff, I won't forget."

He didn't forget. Several months later, he sent me a ticket to one of his fights. I didn't go as you never know what might have happened.

That was an encounter with a man I suppose you would call a sportsman.

The incident just related involved the use of ferrets and "purse" nets, a method usually adopted during the hours of daylight. Most poaching, when conies were plentiful, was carried out at night and usually entailed the use of long nets, normally worked by three men.

It was a dark night in late October. The wind was quite strong and the heavy low clouds were scudding across the sky. Now and again there appeared a gap in the clouds and the light from a town five miles away seemed to be deflected from the open sky and cast a weak glow on the scene. A number of gamekeepers were on duty as it was a favourite type of night for poachers, whether they were after rabbits or pheasants, the latter to be protected at all cost.

As it so happened, the keepers had to get some rabbits and so, whilst guarding the pheasants, they took the opportunity of such a good night for doubling up on the job. The four keepers had set the long nets, six of them, each fifty yards long, and two were setting off to drive the rabbits into the nets. It was what was called a "back set". Normally the nets are set with the wind blowing into them as this way, of course, any noise from the operators was carried away from the feeding rabbits. A "back set" entailed the nets being set close up under a wood, with the wind blowing towards the rabbits, but the sound of the wind in the trees deadening any noise made.

The two keepers went in different directions from the nets, one to the right and one to the left, whilst the other two remained to kill the rabbits as they came in. I was the keeper going to the left and, in order to get behind any conies that may have been out on the large field, I had to make a long detour towards a wood As I got to the wood, a glimmer of light appeared as a gap came in the fast moving clouds. I could see a figure, not far away, and I thought, "That can't be Ron," the other keeper who was driving

I stood still and then I could see that the slowly-moving figure was wearing a trilby on his head, whilst Ron, I knew, was wearing a cap.

Poachers, I thought straight away, as I grabbed for my whistle. Two short and one long blast was the signal for poachers and as I put the whistle to my mouth, I started to run towards the shadowy form.

One short, another short and then I hit the poacher's net. I nearly swallowed my whistle as I almost fell and only a short blast came out. Worse, the man with the trilby had vanished. I recovered my balance and repeated the signal, correctly this time, as I headed along the net the poacher, or poachers, had set.

We stood and listened, but of course the wind deadened most sounds until we heard shouting in the direction of the net we had set. We knew not what we would find, but as we came to a gate out of the field, there were four men, two keepers and two poachers. One of the poachers was rubbing his head, no doubt with due cause, for it appears that one of the keepers made straight for the gate when he heard the signal. After a few moments, two shadowy figures appeared and he leapt out from the gatepost and caught one in each out-stretched hand. They swung round behind him, almost knocking themselves out. The other keeper then appeared and so there was little chance that they would escape. It transpired they also had a mate with them, but he had disappeared completely.

After confiscating all of their tackle and taking their names and addresses, we sent them on their way with one rabbit each, caught in their nets. We then had to pick up our own nets which, to our surprise, held quite a number of rabbits. However, it was getting late, or should I say early in the morning, and so we called it a good night's work and went home.

The poachers were miners from a coal pit about eight miles away, in the Welsh mountains.

To many such people in those days between the wars, poaching was a sport, a way of relaxation after the day's hard work and also, no doubt, they made a few bob, as well as a feed for the family. We were never very hard on them, but naturally we had to make sure they didn't have a free run of the estate, or else pheasants would have been the next thing for the oven.

Another incident occurred at the time I was in lodgings and was regularly cycling to a neighbouring farm every Wednesday evening. It was always in the dark when I left my lodgings since we worked until the light failed and all the pheasants had gone to roost. October arrived and with it the rain. It had been a very dry September and the ground was rock hard, but the rain soaked in and it became possible to easily push the pegs in to set up the long nets for rabbiting. After one or two Wednesday nights away from my patch, I noticed the following morning that there had been some poaching activity.

Here and there could be seen clumps of rabbit fur, various footprints in muddy places and holes where the net pegs had been. Time to do something, I thought, and so I got in touch with the keeper on the adjacent beat and it was decided that the next Wednesday night we would wait and see if the gang paid another visit. The Wednesday night duly came round and we met at an arranged spot, behind a large bush on the edge of a drive, which we were sure the poachers would use.

We remained there for some time, without a word passing between us, and then the distant crunch of tyres on gravel could be heard. George nudged me whispering, "Here they come." The next thing he grabbed my arm and said, "Now". I pulled back and this didn't please George one little bit.

"They'e gone" he said, to which I replied, "Yes I know, but do you know what we have to do tomorrow?".

"No I don't and I don't want to," came his reply. "All I want to do is catch them."

After about half an hour we set off along the drive in the same direction as the "visitors", as George called them.

Eventually we found their cycles, hidden behind a large rhododendron bush and as luck would have it, there was a large piece of tree trunk upon which we could sit and wait.

Time passed, maybe an hour or more, and not a word passed between us for fear we should be heard, but then we could hear the rustling of leaves and even a stick cracking, as the intruders made their way back to their transport. Unaware of our presence, they walked boldly across the drive and came around the bush right to where we were waiting. I jumped up off the log and shouted, "Drop everything."

Down on the ground went the rabbits they had strung round their shoulders on cord.

"Let's have the nets and the pegs," George ordered and the three poachers delved into their large jacket pockets and threw the contents on top of the rabbits. Six fifty-yard nets and a number of pegs were produced and we went through our usual process, taking their names and addresses and giving them instructions that they must pay a pound to the nearest hospital and send a receipt to the Estate Office. With that we then sent them on their way with nothing to show for their night's work and no tackle to enable them to have another go before they got home. George wasn't too pleased when he saw the pile of rabbits.

"Look at that lot," he remarked. "We'll have to walk to the game larder" (which was a good two miles away). We set off along the drive to get our cycles and George was moaning and groaning all the way.

Getting back to the pile of rabbits and nets, I told George that I would hide the nets and pegs under a large yew bush, to collect them in the morning. Meanwhile George was loading the conies onto our propped up cycles. There were rabbits hanging on them everywhere, on the handlebars, on the crossbar and even over the saddle.

"How many do you make it?" I asked my mate.

"I reckon there's eighty-six," came the reply.

"What a pity there's not a few more," I said.

"What do you mean, the bikes wouldn't carry many more, and we've got to push 'em!"

"Never mind George, but do you want to know about tomorrow?"

He replied, "I'm fed up hearing about tomorrow, but I suppose you might as well tell me."

"All right I will. Late this afternoon old Dickie Stark (the Head Keeper) came along the drive in his trap. He said he hadn't seen you, but would I get hold of you and catch a hundred rabbits tomorrow. They are wanted for various folks in town, railway staff, postmen and the like, so now you know what we have to do tomorrow."

"So what?" said George.

"We'll only have to get fourteen now," I told him.

His face lit up. "You crafty devil," he said and from then on he was in a much better mood.

That was a night-time encounter that certainly made the next day's work much easier!

With such large numbers of game birds about, it was inevitable that there would be an odd local who would seize the opportunity of a feed. Not many of the farm labourers of those days dared to touch any game, for it would almost certainly mean instant dismissal, but there were some living in the country who were not in that position.

This encounter involves a "man of the cloth", a vicar who held the living of a church on the edge of the estate. Like many of those times he was a "Sporting Parson", fond of all country pursuits, shooting, fishing and following the hounds, albeit in this case on his bike!

It was a January day and during a spell of cold weather, quite heavy frosts at nights, the sort that, when dawn came, everywhere was white, a hoar frost.

We were spending a few days driving the outlying woods and spinneys after any rabbits that may have been lying out and, at the same time, we were able to ascertain the numbers of pheasants there. This particular small wood was about half a mile from the estate boundary and soon after we started through it, I came across some footprints in the frost. They were not fresh, but must have been made quite recently, for only one or two nights' frost seemed to cover them. I didn't have to detour to follow them, for even when they went to one side or the other, I could keep them in sight. I wondered what the person had been doing in the wood and I didn't have to wait long to find out.

Ahead of me was quite a patch of privet bushes and as I got closer, a number of small birds flew up from the ground and perched in the trees above. There were blackbirds, chaffinches, greenfinches and a variety of "tits", mostly blue tits, and also a moorhen sneaking silently away. I was at once curious and when I got to the shrubs, it was plain to see the reason that so many birds congregated there. The ground was clear of the frost that covered everything, bare soil was showing in places and the fallen leaves had been well disturbed. I looked around and found a hen pheasant's feather and after disturbing some leaves, I discovered a grain of wheat. Someone had been feeding that spot and I was pretty sure I knew why. Not far from the "feed place" I again picked up the footprints which eventually left the wood. In at one end, out at the other.

This person didn't want to give the impression he was going into the wood for a purpose. A couple of days went by and I thought it was time to visit that wood again, just to see if anything had materialised. Quite fresh tracks this time, for the weather was still frosty and they led straight to the privets where I had found the grain of wheat. This time it was different though, for on the site was a cage made of wire-netting, and beneath it there were several handfuls of wheat. The cage was shaped in a fashion that was often used to trap pheasants, but it was not set, being pegged up to allow any birds free passage beneath. It was now quite obvious that someone was intent on catching a few pheasants and more than likely they were quite local.

Two more days passed and I thought it quite possible that the trap was set, so I made it my business to visit the wood again. I approached the clump of privets slowly and when some distance away, I could see a hen pheasant pacing round and round the wire-netting.

Ah, the problem now was, when would that person come to see what he had caught?

It was early afternoon and I calculated that the visit would be made before dusk which would only be in an hour or so, for black clouds lay low in the sky. Only one thing to do..wait!

I found an isolated privet bush some distance from the wire trap and settled down to await the expected visit. After about an hour, I heard a blackbird give its warning call at the end of the wood. A moorhen took off and passed within feet of me and then a figure appeared, moving straight towards the pheasant trap. I had to remain motionless for me to prove anything the poacher had to actually have a pheasant in his hand, or in a sack bag. He came closer to the trap and the hen pheasant started to flutter around and then I could see a cock bird too. The poacher bent down, produced a sack bag from beneath his jacket and soon had both birds safely tied therein. I watched as he reset the trap and was just throwing more wheat, which he produced from his jacket pocket, when I started to sneak up on him. I got within two yards, unheard or seen, and reached forward and tapped him on the shoulder with my stick. He jumped a foot and spun around to face me, no doubt surprised, but not as surprised as I was for it was the local parson, minus his "dog collar".

He didn't know what to say and for that matter neither did I. After a moment or two I said, "Give me that bag vicar, you ought to know better." He handed the bag over saying, "I wasn't going to eat them, I wanted some in a pen. A friend of mine has got a small shoot and he has asked me to rear a few pheasants this year."

"You haven't chosen a very wise way to go about it vicar," I said. "You know I will have to report this."

"I suppose you will," he said, "but it certainly won't happen again."

"Alright," I replied. "Now pull that wire cage up and stamp on it till its useless."

He did this, shaking with apprehension of what would happen I suppose. We eventually walked out of the wood together as the light failed. As he left he said, "God bless you, don't be too hard," and he finished with a quotation which I now can't remember.

After some thought, I decided not to take any action, for I was sure that he wouldn't offend again.

It was about a week later when I was talking to my employer, that the question of poachers cropped up. He asked me if they had been active lately, which at that particular time they hadn't. However, I thought he should know about the incident involving the parson, for I had a good idea that it would probably amuse him.

I related the full story and told him that I had taken no action and did not expect any further offence from the gentleman. His Grace, my employer, said, "You did the right thing, Norman. I would not wish to see a vicar in the dock. I certainly don't like losing my pheasants, but nevertheless I would rather have a parson who poached pheasants than a parson who poached another man's wife."

The latter was a reference to a certain local man of the cloth who had been caught in a compromising situation with a married lady.

To bring this encounter to its final conclusion, it was early May when His Grace called at the laying pens and, of course, was interested in the egg production of the stock birds and also when the first lot of chicks were due out.

As he was leaving, he turned to me and said, "You will have plenty of eggs then, Norman?"

"Oh yes, Your Grace," I replied.

"I just wonder," he added, "if you could spare a hundred or so for the parson who seems so keen on some shooting."

"Certainly," I replied. "That will be no problem. I will get in touch with him and take him the eggs as soon as he has some broody hens ready."

"Jolly good," said His Grace. "Give him my compliments and wish him good sport will you?"

A proper gentleman if ever there was one!

Sometimes, of course, poachers were not treated so leniently although, by and large, locals who only took the odd bird when the opportunity occurred, were given only a stern warning and rarely offended again. This case was a bit different. It concerned a farm worker who had only been in the employ of this particular farmer for a matter of months. Close to the stockyard of the farm was a wood, which had been planted a number of years and was a favourite resort of numerous pheasants. At the time of planting, there were vast numbers of rabbits about and to save the young trees from their champing teeth, the wood was surrounded with small mesh wire-netting. Any pheasant outside of the wood used to run up and down the field, bobbing at the netting until they took it into their heads to fly over. It was October time and on my rounds one day, I noticed a small area against the netting that had been disturbed and, upon investigation, I found a couple of small feathers from a pheasant. After scraping some of the leaves and loose grass away, I could see traces of some sort of feed. This evidence warned me that some person was throwing something down to attract the game birds.

The next visit to this spot only served to confirm what I thought. Lying there was a quantity of what obviously was broken up "cattle nuts". The oily mixture in this sort of feed would certainly be very attractive to pheasants. What to do now, that was the problem. I knew not who was responsible, but it was almost certainly someone from the adjacent farm, but who?

There was only one way to find out and that was to wait in the wood until the culprit appeared. Knowing that the spot had been fed that day, I decided to be in the wood out of sight the next morning, when the staff had their break after milking. The milking machine engine stopped turning and the cattle could be seen going down the farm lane to a pasture.

"Won't be long now," I thought.

Time passed and nothing happened until the tractors started up after the breakfast break, but before they moved off, a man came and looked over the stockyard gate in the direction of the wood. I recognised him as a worker who had only been employed on the farm a few months. He stared for a while and then I could hear the tractor moving off. "Not today, but the time will come," I thought.

After several more fruitless waits, I was getting a bit fed up and decided to go and see the farmer whilst the men were away working in the fields. I explained my predicament and suspicions.

"I reckon you're right," said the farmer. "I thought there was something shifty about him just recently."

"Any suggestions?" I asked the farmer, whose family had tenanted the farm for several generations.

"I'll tell 'ee what," he said, "'tis the ploughing and hedge laying match on Wednesday. Yon mon will be the only one on the farm 'tween milking I'll see to that."

"Right, thanks," I replied for by now several pheasants had found the food against the wire and spent a lot of time there.

The Wednesday duly arrived and around nine thirty I was in the wood, hiding behind a big bush not far from where I could see several pheasants feeding against the wire. I hadn't been in position very long before I could pick out a figure climbing over the stockyard gate, only to be followed by another. They stood a few minutes and I could see one gesticulating, his arm pointing one way then another. They moved off, one going one way and the other in the opposite direction. It was obvious they were going to corner those birds on that patch of briars against the wire.

I watched and waited. One of the cock pheasants close to me, outside the wire, put its head up and started to move. They're close now, I thought, and the next moment I could see, and hear, pheasants taking to the wing. "That's it," I said to myself, "they've missed them," but then I heard the obvious sound of a briar clump being thrashed with a stick, or as it turned out, with sticks. I moved my position slightly and as I did so, saw the elder man grab a cock pheasant out of the now demolished clump of briars. I jumped up, vaulted over the low fence and I have never seen such a look of surprise. They were caught red-handed, one with a pheasant in his hand and it was no use running for I knew who they were. There was nothing they could say. They just stood there with their mouths wide open, but they weren't very happy either when told they would be prosecuted for taking game and, of course, the farmer they worked for would have to be told.

That afternoon when the farmer and his staff got back from the ploughing, just about milking time, I made it my business to be around. I gave the old lad a chance to change into his working clothes and met him on his way across the cobbled yard to the shippons.

"Any luck?" he greeted me with.

"Yes," I replied, "and it wasn't long after you left for the ploughing match."

"I'm pleased," he said, "I canna bear having a wrong 'un about the place."

"Ah, but there were two," I told him, "One was that youngish bloke you've only had here a week or two." The farmer "wizened" a bit and then said, "The crafty sod. He said this morning that he couldn't afford to come with us and would rather stop and finish ploughing the "twenty acre", ready to sow wheat."

"Aye, he did go there after I had dealt with them," I told the farmer.

"Well tell us what happened then," the old lad said, so I explained the situation to him.

"You'll be taking them to court, I reckon," he said. "Best thing you can do, let others know they canna' get away with it."

"That's what will happen mester," I replied.

"Now I wunna say 'owt to 'em, let 'em stew. They may get the idea they've got away with it," added the farmer.

In due course, after making the usual statement to the powers-that-be, the pair of them were up before the local magistrates. They both had the sense to plead guilty and after some deliberation by the Bench, they were fined the maximum at that time, £10 each. Neither of them asked for time to pay, as so often happened in cases of this kind.

Afterwards they were waiting outside the Magistrates Court when I came out and when I saw them I wondered what they had in mind, but was not greatly concerned, for I was in the company of the local police constables.

As we approached, the pair stepped forward and the elder one said to me, "It was a fair cop, we should have known better," and the constable replied, "Aye you should, but you've paid the price."

The younger of the pair added, "One thing's sure, I wunna touch a pheasant or even a rabbit ever again."

They both shook hands with the constable and myself and left after remarking, "We wunna bear any grudges."

Knowing the farmer, and for that matter his terms of tenancy from the estate, I reckoned that there would be more to come for the erring couple. I did pay a visit or two to the wood where the offence had taken place, but all was well, no signs of any more feeding activities, but I did not go near the farm on these occasions. It was a week or two later that I met the farmer and a stranger with him.

"You haven't met Joe, have you?" he said. "Well I dare say you knows I got rid of those other pair, and glad to get shut tell 'ee the truth. This fellow won't touch 'owt, will 'ee Joe? T'aint allowed on my place."

"Well I hope you're here a long while Joe," I said. "You've got a good boss. He's a "straight" 'un, so long as you're straight with him. No doubt I'll see you about."

It seemed strange to me but, soon after the law was passed to protect badgers, we had gangs arriving with their terriers to dig "brock" out. There were quite a number of badger setts, and for that matter still are, on the estate. On several occasions I had come across setts that had been disturbed, but this was only after it was illegal to touch them. However, I was having my lunch one day, when one of the farmers phoned to say he had seen four men with terriers, crossing his land and one of these men was carrying a spade. "Are you interested?" he asked.

"Of course," I replied as I queried the precise location where he had last seen them.

"Were they heading for the Pied Clump?" I enquired.

"Aye, more or less," he said.

I thanked him and put the phone down. It seemed pretty obvious what they were going to do and so I contacted the local bobby and we agreed a plan of action. He said he would arrange for one of his colleagues to come from a certain direction when he received instructions over his radio and I suggested we met in a nearby village out of sight of the Pied Clump. In a short while, I was on my way to the rendezvous and as I passed the clump in question, driving along the main road, I glanced across, and sure enough a white and tan terrier showed itself on the grass field. My friend, the local bobby soon arrived, but in his own car so that the presence of a police vehicle would not give the game away.

He contacted the other officer on his personal radio and in a short while the trap was set.

We were to approach the clump from three different directions, making it almost certain that we should catch one or two of the gang. I could see the policeman crossing the fields. It was his job to spring the trap and sure enough, when he was about thirty yards from the small wood, three men came out on our side. They split up, one coming towards where I was out of sight, and the other two towards the hidden policeman. When the man running towards me was about ten yards away, I popped up and shouted, "Stop!"

He paused and then took off again with me in pursuit! Fortunately for me, after a short distance, he gave up completely winded. I grabbed him by the arm and looked round to see how the local policeman had fared. As I watched him in full flight after one of the men, I could see another sitting on a fence and this puzzled me. Still holding the sleeve of the man I had got, we made our way towards the one sitting on the fence and I could still see the policeman chasing the third man. The man trying to evade capture managed to crawl through a hedge with the chasing "arm of the law" only a yard or two behind. With one terrific leap the policeman jumped the hedge and I could see his helmet going up in the air, almost like a flying saucer.

Eventually, in four or five strides he came up to the man he was chasing and with one shove had him on the ground. We all gathered in one place and it appeared that the one I'd seen sitting on the fence was known to the local police and decided to save his breath and not try to run away. There were terriers milling round us, some jumping up to the men we had captured and then it dawned on me. The farmer said he had seen four men.

"Where's the other?" I thought, but I didn't ask the terrier men. Instead I asked how many dogs they had with them.

"Six," said the man known to the local police, but I could only count five.

"Where's the other one," I asked.

"Down the fox hole," he muttered.

The policeman who had sprung the trap said, "I'll go and look see," and headed for Pied Clump. In a short while he was returning with another man and a dog.

Well they were all caught and in due course appeared before the local magistrates. They claimed, as has happened in so many badger digging cases since, that it was a fox earth, not a badger sett, but the magistrates accepted my evidence that it had been a badger sett for many years, and it was almost certain that badgers were in residence when the accused were caught there.

They were all convicted and fined the maximum amount and after the proceedings, a senior police officer told me that it was only the second case under the new Act in the country. It certainly wasn't my last encounter with badger diggers though.

*****

During my Army service through the Second World War, I was for the whole period in the Royal Artillery, starting in a light anti-aircraft regiment. As time went by and a number of moves later, from gunsite to gunsite, mainly in Lancashire, I found myself as a batman to a Major, at Brigade Headquarters.

After quite a short period, the Major told me we were moving to Nottingham where he was taking up the position of A.D.C. to the general of the 5th Ack Ack

Group. This in itself was unusual as the correct and normal rank for A.D.C. to a General was Captain.

It came to my knowledge in due course, that the General was a regular army man and would have been retired but for the war and the Major was in the Territorial Army and would also have retired but for the war.

The A.D.C., Major Wray, was a kindly gentleman, and a countryman too and one day he told me he chose me as his batman because in civvy street I was a gamekeeper and he hoped, given the chance, to do a bit of fishing and shooting. The Major was very disappointed when the General's batman was discharged on medical grounds and I had to take over the position of looking after General Frith, but there wasn't much he could do about that. The General was a man who loved country pursuits and wanted me for the same reason!

Not far from the Group Headquarters at Nottingham, there was quite a sizeable lake, or perhaps to be more correct, a large pond. It appeared to be man-made and the General had heard there were trout in this water. A fishing expedition was arranged, but on arriving at the site, the water didn't look to me as if it would have many trout in it. After many many 'casts', expertly done, I might add, by both officers, there wasn't the slightest sign of a fish. I was staring all the time at the calm water and after an hour or more, I saw the surface of the water broken and a large fish showed its fins for a few seconds.

It was obviously a pike - and not a small one at that. I drew the Major's attention to it, for I was standing close to him at the time. That was the end of the fishing that day!

A few day's later, the General asked me if the "lake" would hold trout if the pike were removed. I told him that in my opinion it would. There was a watercourse draining into the pond, although only small, and a spill way out, but the problem would be catching the pike!

After thinking a bit he said: "No problem. We'll get

REME (Royal Electrical and Mechanical Engineers) to chuck a few explosives in and gather the pike up."

Well, it is well known that an explosion under water will bring fish to the surface, though mostly only stunned and it would need some sharpish activity to gather the pike. Nobody knew how many there were.

In due course all arrangements had been made and the 'Explosion Gang' arrived, one officer and a sergeant, plus a small boat!

Into the lake went several charges, one after the other, with the water and mud going at least thirty feet into the air. I bet the local residents thought it was 'Jerry' on a daylight bombing raid.

When the water settled, there were a number of fish on the surface and the sergeant and myself set off in the boat to collect them. I cannot recall the total, but it was not a large number, mainly pike of up to about ten pounds and some smaller fish which I believed to be rudd.

There was a fair old smell from all the disturbed mud, but after waiting a while before making another sweep of the water and not finding another fish, the general was satisfied the lake was clear of pike and declared that it had been a good evening's work.

I wasn't quite so sure the water was pike free, but in due course it was arranged that some trout should be turned into the water. I don't know how many, I was not present on that occasion.

Quite a number of evening visits were made in an attempt to attract the fish to a fly, but all were without success and I reckon the whole operation provided a few feeds for any herons in the area!

General Frith and Major Wray were both keen on country pursuits and that meant mainly fishing in the summer and shooting in the winter. All personnel on Ack Ack were allowed to have a day pass of sixteen hours once a week - and this applied to officers and other ranks - so most weeks the General and A.D.C. would be either fishing or shooting according to the season.

These expeditions meant a certain amount of travelling and the drill was to travel say on a Wednesday, visiting and inspecting gunsites and searchlight sites, finishing the day usually at Regimental Headquarters, where the General and A.D.C. would have dinner and stop the night. The driver, Corporal Jones, and myself, would have a feed in the sergeants' mess and sleep in their quarters.

Corporal Jones had driven the General of Western Command for a number of years and was a very experienced regular soldier. I well remember my first sporting trip. We were due to leave HQ at seven thirty a.m. and it was barely light. All was loaded up and the two officers appeared, the General carrying a map. He put the map on the bonnet of the car, stubbed his finger on it and said, "Jones, that's where I want to go."

"Very good, Sir," came the reply. Now during the war, it must be remembered, there were no signposts, no road numbers, in fact nothing to aid navigation.

We set off with me having no idea where we were going, just enjoying the scenery once we got out of the urban area. After about an hour on the road, Corporal Jones turned down a country lane and after travelling a mile or more, a searchlight site loomed up in front of us. How the Corporal navigated his way I shall never know. Just one quick glance in not very good light at the army map and he drove straight there!

Several more calls were made to gun sites etcetera, all found with just a quick look at the map, and in due course we arrived at R.H.Q. somewhere in Yorkshire. It was here that we were to spend the night. I realised that there was to be some sort of a shoot the next day as we had shotguns in the car and there was, on the General's instructions, a suit of plus fours in his luggage.

The evening was spent in the sergeants' mess after quite a substantial meal.

The morning dawned quite bright and with just a gentle breeze, a pleasant sort of day to be shooting. I knew quite well that game birds were unlikely to be around in large numbers for the war had put a stop to the rearing of pheasants, partridge and mallard. However, I was looking forward to the day's activities.

After a good breakfast, we moved off, but not far, for after ten minutes or so, the A.D.C. said: "Next turning on the right, Corporal." So the Major was now in familiar territory, but Corporal Jones knew where to go all right - the General had pointed it out on a map!

On arrival at what was really quite a moderate sized country house, we were met by several men, obviously ready for the day's shooting. After quite a bit of chattering amongst the gentlemen, we moved off down an overgrown footpath until we arrived at a fair sized wood. It appeared to be at least thirty acres, perhaps more. It was oak and ash in the main, with small areas of softwood and plenty of undergrowth, the type of wood-land much loved by pheasants.

There was only one dog between the five shots, a rather obese and aged spaniel which I couldn't see doing much hunting in the patchy but dense cover.

The party lined up and started down the wood, which because of its contour had to be walked half at a time. As expected, there was not much shooting. A few rabbits were killed, a pheasant and a woodcock missed and much to my relief, the General had two shots at a hare without effect (had he killed it, I would have had to have carried it!). So the morning passed, walking through some woods and spinneys, not finding much game to shoot at, but not having much to carry either.

A short break was made to enjoy a sandwich lunch and a bottle of ale and then we continued walking over some rough, boggy terrain where quite a number of snipe were found. To my surprise, one gentleman shot four without a miss. (Not heavy to carry anyway). We were now walking through a narrow belt of trees on a steep slope. This was flanked on one side by a main road with open land the other side of the trees.

A pheasant was heard to call as it took off and appeared about twenty yards in front of the General heading as if to cross the road and making for lower ground. Quite a sporting shot, I thought, and with a single shot, the General brought it crashing to the ground, or rather onto the road below us. At that moment as I moved off to retrieve it, a bus appeared and stopped right by the dead bird. Out jumped the driver who picked up the pheasant and held it at arm's length, as so many people do. He looked up the slope towards us, jumped in the cab and drove off!

The General raised his hat as the bus moved off, turned to me and said: "I hope he enjoys it. I don't suppose he has tasted it before."

"Probably not, Sir. But I hope he has got a file," I replied.

"File, file, what do you mean, man?"

"Well, I reckon he'll need a file to sharpen his teeth. That bird had a tail a yard long, two or three-years-old at least, tough as old boots!"

"Ha, ha, ha!" was the General's reponse. "Good luck to him, eh?"

At the end of the day, the small bag was shared out. It did run to a brace of pheasants and a rabbit or two apiece, but I'm sure a good day was had by all. The spoils were loaded into the car and the General said: "Home, Jones," and almost immediately went to sleep.

It was by now dark and the car had very little in the way of lights. The headlights were covered so that only a small slit let any light out and it was a job to see the road, let alone anything else. We trundled on at what had to be a slow pace, passing through villages and a small town.

In due course, we arrived back at headquarters and as the car stopped, the General woke up and said: "Jolly good show, eh what? Thank-you Jones." The A.D.C. was still asleep, but woke as we unloaded and disappeared into the officers' mess. All I can say is, I think Corporal Jones' navigation, under those circumstances, was nothing less than marvellous.

Country
Characters

These days, it is pretty rare to see an aged country-man leaning on the gate to his abode. Years ago, you could go round any village on a lovely evening in spring or summer and be certain to come across several of these gentlemen. Many of them would be hoping for someone to come along and have a chat, and most interesting chats they could be. Some, of course, were very taciturn and could hardly pass the time of day with even local people and any strangers were definitely "up to no good". This story is about one of those who loved to have a chat, or pass the time of day.

It was a late spring evening, fresh and with the birds full of song as the swallows swirled about the sky. As I cycled along the lane I could hear, in an adjacent hay field, a corncrake calling its rasping call, alas heard no longer these days. Not far away, on the water meadows, a peewit was performing aerial acrobatics as its dulcet notes filled the air. I turned the corner and there, leaning on his cottage "wicket" (gate) was Tom. I was in no great hurry, so I stopped for a few words, getting as always from Tom, "How be?" as a greeting.

We discussed the weather, always on the agenda that, and various goings on in the village. After a while Tom glanced down the road and said: "Hey up, here comes old Horace". This gentleman's farm was only about a hundred yards away and doubtless he had spotted us talking and came to join in, hoping no doubt to get a bit of local news. He was dubbed "The Chronicle" by all the locals, so that indicates his leanings. Horace was about

116

twenty yards away when he shouted, "Anna you heard?".

"Heard what?" Tom replied.

"Old Thomas up Shropshire way has gone "jed" and left twenty six thousand, so many hundreds and one penny".

"Nay he hasn't left that!" was Tom's response.

"I'm telling you he has!" was Horace's emphatic response.

"Yea didna know him did you, Tom?"

"No not me, but I know he didn't leave all that money."

"I'm telling you he did."

"Nay he didna."

The Chronicle was getting fed up by now; he didn't like being contradicted.

"I'll go and get the paper and show ye," he said as he started back down the footpath to his farm.

He hadn't got very far when Tom shouted, "Hey Horace, come back for a moment. He didn't leave it you know, Horace, he was taken from it!"

"Aye, they be right mon, I reckon he'd rather still be here, dunna you?"

This seemed to me to be pretty sound logic, for whether it is thousands of pounds, or only a hundred or two, who wants to leave it?

Talking of money reminds me of Billy the joiner who literally put his shirt on going to the races. It was the custom for estate workers to have half a day to go to Chester Races and Billy rushed home to get changed, to be there in good time for the Chester Cup. His wife had laid everything out for him in readiness, but he couldn't find his braces. "You've hidden the damn things," he roared. "You never wanted me to go in the first place."

"Yes I did," said his wife. "And I wanted you to put a bob on for me."

Billy looked everywhere, but to no avail, and eventually it was too late. He sat down in the chair, not in the best of moods. Some time later his wife said, "What's keeping your trousers up, Billy?" Billy jumped up to find that he had put his braces on after all, and his shirt over the top! He didn't get to the races, but maybe had the last laugh. The horse that he was going to back didn't win the Chester Cup, but his wife's did, and at odds of ten to one!

Quite a few of the landlords in country pubs had a dry sense of humour. I suppose this was, in those distant days, one thing that was essential. Frequented by local farmers, who have always been reputed to be moaners, it was essential to be able to cheer up the atmosphere a bit on a miserable winter's night, probably reasoning that if you could get the clients in a better frame of mind, they would be more likely to "sup" a drop more ale.

This particular evening, there were rather more in the bar than usual, and Joe the landlord was, for him, quite busy. The evening was wearing on, when a couple of local lads could be seen through the bar window and the haze of smoke from fags and pipes.

"Hey up," somebody said. "Here comes old Sam's son and his mate."

Old Sam was at a table in the corner playing dominoes with his friend and couldn't see through the window, his sight wasn't too good anyway.

"He said he'd come," remarked Sam. "With a bit of luck he'll buy me a pint."

In due course the door opened and in walked two youths who went straight up to the bar, where old Joe was having an argument with his wife.

"Thee stay in the kitchen woman, I'll stay in the bar," he could be heard saying.

He turned to greet the new customers, for he had heard the door as they came in. Looking at the pair closely he said, "What does they want?".

"Two pints of mild please Mr Lloyd," said one of them.

"Are they old enough to sup ale?" asked the landlord.

"Oh yes," said one. "Ask me dad, he's over there."

Old Joe took another look at the pair and one of them asked, "What's the matter Mr Lloyd?".

"I'll tell thee what's the matter. If they canna afford to get thee hair cut, thee canna afford to sup ale in my pub", for both of the youngsters had long hair, way down on their shoulders, which was then the fashion.

"Can I buy my dad a drink then?" the youth asked. "Nay ye canna. He can buy his own," with which Joe shepherded the lads to the door!

It was in the same hostelry, "The Boot" at Willington, in Cheshire, that another encounter occurred. For many years it was the custom for several of the local men to gather, once or twice a week, for a game of dominoes, which was a favourite pastime in village pubs at one time. There was usually a local builder, one of his employees and a couple of farm men, one of which was an Irishman, long domiciled in the area. Many a night this innocent pastime had taken place, but eventually, either through death or age, this gang got smaller, but one or two others took their place and thus the old tradition of playing the "spots", as they called it, continued. One corner of the pub was more or less earmarked for these locals and seldom did another person use it.

When the "gang" were playing it was an education to watch their faces, as the smoke curled up to the knarled oak beams in the ceiling. Sheer concentration caused them, on more than one occasion, to knock their glass of ale as they reached out for a sip, but I never did see any ale "shed", the movement was too slow for that! It was easy to tell when they had the game "stitched up" as they called it, by the faint smile that appeared on a weather-worn face. Such was the concentration that now and again, they wouldn't even hear the landlord call time. It was ten o'clock then, but so long as there were no glasses on the table, he would let them finish the game.

"Rag and Bone" men were frequent visitors to rural areas and their familiar cry would be heard as soon as they got near any habitation. They would visit regularly and it must have been a profitable business as their expenses were negligible, for the horse or pony was fed on the grass verges and any open spaces during the day's journey. The "shandry", or small "flat -bottomed cart", usually without side boards, needed little care, and on top of that, many country wives would offer them a cup of tea and maybe a chunk of bread and a piece of cheese. The man was fed, the horse was fed, and the only expense was a copper or two for any old clothes or bones.

The old lad in question, like many of them, was pretty crafty and always arranged his visits during the school holidays when the children would be playing on the village green and around the country lanes.

He didn't seem to shout quite so loud if he could see the kids playing, but would always ask them, "Has your mother got any old clothes? I'll take some bones too."

Of course the children dashed home and many of them would return with very old clothes, many of which showed more patches than the original material, and some would be clutching a bone in already grimy hands. The Rag and Bone man would make a big show of inspecting the goods the children had brought, throwing some aside saying, "That b'aint any use to me".

This brought a frown to a child's face, for it thought there would be nothing forthcoming. The bones were always accepted straight away and put in a bag on the cart, then of course came the time to settle the bargain. For an old jumper and maybe an over-darned pair of socks, there would be a balloon, but the prize all the children hankered for was a goldfish. On the cart would be a big glass jar and the silver and gold fish could be plainly seen swimming round and round in their con-fined space. Alongside would be a number of glass jam jars in an old wooden box. Now if a youngster produced a big pile of old clothing, he stood a good chance of seeing one of the small jars filled with water and a wriggling fish popped in. A prize indeed!

There was a ready market for bones as there was a glue factory only a few miles away, so on his way home the Rag man could sell what he had gathered during the day. It so happened that not far from this glue factory, which was well out in the country because of the smell which issued from its chimney, was an old country pub.

The Rag man had had a good day and having a load of bones to dispose of, had been to the factory and collected his money. As it was early in the afternoon, the hostelry was still open, so he made his way there, well pleased with the day's work and the cash in his pocket.

Of course, he had to secure his horse before he could enter the establishment. He did not intend to stay long, so deemed it unnecessary to unharness the animal and put it in one of the stables, so, as there was a gate leading into a field at the back of the pub, he tied the horse to this. There were several locals in the public bar and they were soon in animated conversation with the Rag man. Time went by and more and more ale was supped, as for once, the Rag man felt generous.

Closing time was approaching, when two younger members of the group left the bar and it was assumed that they were following a "call of nature". But they also had other plans! Going out onto the back yard of the pub, they found the Rag man's horse and got it free of the cart shafts. As one led the horse a few yards away, the other lowered the shafts to the ground and then opened the gate into the field. His mate then led the horse through and the gate was shut, leaving the horse on one side and the cart on the other. Next the shafts of the cart were put through the bars of the field gate and soon the horse was safely backed into them and all the leather straps fastened.What a situation, the horse in the cart, but a field gate between them! Hurrying back into the pub, the pair of pranksters had a job to keep a straight face, but made a great effort as they joined the party at the bar.

By now, the Rag and Bone man was getting quite merry, but nevertheless the two who had been so busy thought it might be a good idea to buy the old lad a drop of whisky, maybe then he wouldn't be quite so enraged when he got to his means of transport.

The landlord called "time" and soon the prank was

being explained to those not in the know who then quickly disappeared to a vantage point where they could see but would be unseen. The victim shortly put in an appearance, standing on the steps, blinking his eyes as they met the bright sunshine, and, once accustomed to that, he moved off round the corner of the building. It was obvious he was not aware of the situation, for he climbed up to his seat, picked the reins up and started by saying "Whoa", then "Back up, me lad".

After several repetitions of this, and all that was happening was that the horse was getting pretty uneasy, he must have remembered that he had not undone the cord which he had tied to the gate. Stumbling as he dismounted from the cart, he made towards the horse's head. He couldn't get to the horse's head - the gate was in the way! He stood, took off his cap, scratched his head, replaced his cap, went round the back of the cart, came to the gate again, removed his cap and did some more scratching. The concealed onlookers were in stitches of laughter, it was a wonder they didn't give away their place of concealment. Eventually, one of the pranksters went to the aid of the Rag man and asked, "Did your 'oss get through t'gate?" This prompted the old lad to start ranting and raving, but he soon cooled down when some of the lads unhinged the gate.

He hadn't the slightest idea that his rescuers were the culprits. "I know it wasn't yea lot," he said. "I've been with you all afternoon, reckon it was someone local though". Thinking of the amount the old lad had supped, one of the lads asked, "Will you get home alright?"

"Oh aye," was the reply. "T'hoss has taken me home many a time" and he lifted the reins and set off out of the pub yard at quite a gallop.

The locals stood laughing about this incident when the local bobby appeared and the incident was related to him. "Well I'll be damned," he said. "There was a horse and cart going like the clappers, they met me up the lane. I thought the old lad slumped in the seat looked familiar."

No-one can remember the Rag man calling at that particular pub again!

Life in one way or another is full of encounters, some remain in one's memory for many, many years, others are soon forgotten. I have recalled quite a few which have come my way, but there are a lot more, in themselves only small events but which still remain with me after such a long time. All those which I have related actually happened, although I don't seem to have written very much about the ladies. I can assure you it hasn't been a deliberate omission, but somehow they, at least in bygone years, did not seem to be so prominent in day-to-day goings on. They stopped at home and looked after the children!!!

However, I will try and make up for it and write about a girl called Eileen who was born in Chester and was christened in Chester Cathedral. Owing to her mother dying quite young, she had to move with her father and the rest of the family to live in Holt, the first village in Wales, over Farndon Bridge. The family lived about a mile the other side of Holt, on a rather isolated lane. Holt, particularly in those days, was well known, in fact I will go as far as to say 'famous' for strawberry growing. Things have changed a bit since the 1920s when many acres and many gardens too, were covered with strawberry plants. The fruit is still grown today, but on a much smaller scale. In the Twenties, gangs of workers used to invade Holt when the fruit was ripe, round about June time, and practically all ladies and children in the village would get involved too.

So it is quite understandable that once out of school and at weekends, it was a great attraction to get into the strawberry fields and help gather the crop. I don't think the children earned much money and many probably had to hand over their earnings to their mother, for they were hard times. Of course, Our Eileen was no different than any of the other kids and spent as much time as possible in the strawberry fields. At the end of the season, when the bulk of the crop had been gathered, the farmers used to let the local people gather the remains of the crop, by now rather small and unsellable, for jam-making and no doubt that is what happened to the fruit, but not all of it in the immediate area, for once the locals had enough for their own use, the rest was sold on.

So here comes our young Eileen again. Accompanying her elder brother, she had helped him gather a considerable amount of these small strawberries in baskets they had found in the field. There were always some around which had blown away with the wind. A short way out of Holt on their way home there was a fork in the road and the two youngsters decided to stay there and try and sell the baskets of fruit to passers-by. There weren't many cars in those days, but in due course, all but one basket had been sold.

"We had better take one basket home," said her brother, Bill, and they wended their way up the winding lane. Before they got to their gate, Eileen said: "What about the money, Bill?"

"Oh yes," replied Bill. "Mother will want it off us if she knows."

After some thought, he came up with the idea of burying it and chose a gate post to be the hiding place. Some soil was scooped out and the money, not very much I guess, was duly buried.

"I know what we will do with that," said Bill. "We'll spend it when we go on the Sunday School outing to Rhyl in a week or two."

The day arrived and the pair of them went to gather their money, but despite all their searching, not a copper could be found and they had to leave it or miss the coach! Many attempts were made to locate the missing money, but not a coin was ever found. I went past the spot some time ago and wondered if a metal detector would come up trumps. Maybe in the distant future the hoard will be discovered and the finders will wonder what 'foreign' currency they have found!

In due course, Eileen, like most girls of her generation, had to go into service. Some went into large houses as maids of one sort or another, but many country girls had to accept a post on a farm where the duties could be varied, from cleaning the house, helping with the milking, working in the fields or in the dairy. As it so happened, Eileen spent most of her time in the dairy, for the farm she was on was a dairy farm, producing a large amount of milk that was made into cheese on the premises. The maids had a certain amount of time off, depending on the whim of their employer. Most villages had regular dances in the village halls, sixpenny hops, they called them, and this incident happened after such an evening.

Eileen and another maid had been to a village about two miles from where they worked and when it was over, around midnight, Eileen found she then had to face the bike ride down the lonely country lanes on her own, her friend having got a young lad to take her home. However, Eileen persuaded a friend to let her borrow her boyfriend to escort her to the farm. All went well until the lad's carbide lamp became flooded and Eileen's oil lamp was but a dim glow. They pressed on despite the darkness of the night and on reaching the farm drive, her borrowed escort said: "You'll be all right now," and he turned around and headed back home.

Eileen put her cycle in the usual place and went upstairs to bed. Hardly had the candle been lit, when the pebbles rained against the window. She knew at once who it was – a local chap a lot older than herself who had been pestering her at every opportunity. She opened the window and shouted: "Get off, Dan, I know it's you. I don't want anything to do with you."

A voice replied: "If you won't have anything to do with me, I'll throw myself in the river."

"Go on then and good riddance," she replied.

All went quiet, but the next morning, the farmer met Eileen and asked: "Why did you put your bike on that bacon hook in the dairy ceiling?"

Of course the tale of the pebble thrower came out and it was concluded that Dan was the culprit. He was the reason why Eileen was so desperate to have an escort home from the dance, but despite her worries that he might carry out his threat about the river, he was still around for a long time, but there were no more incidents with Dan.

Eventually, Eileen decided that the time had come to move on, mainly because the maid that she started work with was leaving and the replacement was well known to be a bit of a tyrant. Another farm or a different job? There weren't a lot of choices in those days, but as Eileen had been helping out with the cheesemaking, she came to the conclusion that that was the job she would like to do. It was not just a case of applying for a cheesemaker's job. No farmer would give an unqualified person a thought. There was only one way and that was to go to an agricultural college and pass the required exams.

In those days, most counties had such colleges, but it was very costly to go to one in a county other than where you lived or at least worked. Eileen had been working just over the border in Wales, so the college she was able to go to was at Ruthin, Llysfasi Dairy School.

There were quite a number of young ladies as students, mostly Welsh, and farmer's daughters, but Eileen soon settled in. It was the custom for the girls to attend church on Sundays, but Eileen was at rather a loss, for every other Sunday, the service was in Welsh.

This particular Sunday, a party of girls were at the church for the fortnightly English service and in due course the plate came round for the collection. Eileen's friend, next to her whispered: "I haven't got any money". "Oh dear," whispered Eileen, "I'll lend you some."

She put her hand in her pocket and gave her friend twopence as, apparently, this was the usual amount put on the plate by the girls. Eileen was sure she had some more money, but as the collector approached, she realised all she had was half a crown. There was nothing to be done but to put the coin on the plate where it shone out like a star amongst the coppers.

After the service, the girls gathered outside and